Horace Satires

The following titles are available from Bloomsbury for the
OCR specifications in Latin and Greek for examinations from
June 2019 to June 2021

Apuleius *Metamorphoses* V: A Selection, with introduction, commentary
notes and vocabulary by Stuart Thomson

Cicero *Philippic* II: A Selection, with introduction, commentary notes and
vocabulary by Christopher Tanfield

Horace *Odes:* A Selection, with introduction, commentary notes and
vocabulary by John Godwin

Horace *Satires:* A Selection, with introduction, commentary notes and
vocabulary by John Godwin

Ovid *Amores* II: A Selection, with introduction, commentary notes and
vocabulary by Alfred Artley

Tacitus *Histories* I: A Selection, with introduction
by Ellen O'Gorman and commentary notes and vocabulary
by Benedict Gravell

Virgil *Aeneid* XI: A Selection, with introduction, commentary notes and
vocabulary by Ashley Carter

OCR Anthology for Classical Greek AS and A Level, covering the
prescribed texts by Aristophanes, Euripides, Herodotus, Homer,
Plato and Xenophon, with introduction, commentary notes and vocabulary
by Stephen P. Anderson, Rob Colborn, Neil Croally, Charlie Paterson,
Chris Tudor and Claire Webster

Supplementary resources for these volumes can be found at
www.bloomsbury.com/OCR-editions-2019-2021
Please type the URL into your web browser and follow
the instructions to access the Companion Website.
If you experience any problems, please contact
Bloomsbury at academicwebsite@bloomsbury.com

Horace *Satires*:
A Selection

I.1 lines 1–12, 28–100; I.3 lines 25–75; II.2 lines 1–30, 70–111

With introduction, commentary
notes and vocabulary
by John Godwin

BLOOMSBURY ACADEMIC
LONDON • NEW YORK • OXFORD • NEW DELHI • SYDNEY

BLOOMSBURY ACADEMIC
Bloomsbury Publishing Plc
50 Bedford Square, London, WC1B 3DP, UK

BLOOMSBURY, BLOOMSBURY ACADEMIC and the
Diana logo are trademarks of Bloomsbury Publishing Plc

First published in Great Britain 2018
Reprinted 2019

Cover image: charistoone-images / Alamy Stock Photo

Bloomsbury Publishing Plc does not have any control over, or responsibility
for, any third-party websites referred to or in this book. All internet
addresses given in this book were correct at the time of going to press. The
author and publisher regret any inconvenience caused if addresses have
changed or sites have ceased to exist, but can accept no responsibility for
any such changes.

A catalogue record for this book is available from the British Library.

Library of Congress Cataloging-in-Publication Data
A catalogue record for this book is available from the Library of Congress.

ISBN: PB: 978-1-3500-0036-0
ePDF: 978-1-3500-0038-4
eBook: 978-1-3500-0037-7

Typeset by Integra Software Services Pvt. Ltd.
Printed and bound in India

To find out more about our authors and books visit www.bloomsbury.com
and sign up for our newsletters.

Contents

Preface

This book is intended to assist students preparing for public examinations in Latin who are required to study this text, but it can of course be used by any students of Latin who have mastered the basics and who are now ready to start reading some Latin verse and developing their skills and their understanding. The notes assume that the reader has studied the Latin language roughly as far as GCSE, but the vocabulary list glosses every word in the text and the Introduction assumes that the reader is coming to Horace for the very first time. To assist with the comprehension of the Latin, the vocabulary at the end of the book includes line references to places where a particular word has a different meaning from the one found in basic dictionaries, and it is worth consulting the vocabulary whenever the meaning is not fully explained in the commentary. Tricky phrases are explained and translated in the commentary and it is important that the student also uses the vocabulary to be certain of the meaning of every word so that the music and the emphases of the verse can be fully appreciated. The commentary seeks to elucidate the background and the literary features of this highly artistic text, while also helping the reader to understand how the Latin words fit together into their sentences.

My thanks are due above all to Alice Wright and her team at Bloomsbury who have been a model of efficiency and enthusiasm and a delight to write for. My thanks also go to Dr Emily Gowers of St John's College, Cambridge and the two anonymous readers from the publishers and from OCR respectively who both read the whole of this book in draft form and made many highly useful comments which saved me from error as well as pointing me towards a better reading of the text.

John Godwin
Shrewsbury 2017

Introduction

Horace and his times

Horace was born into a world on the verge of dramatic change. When Quintus Horatius Flaccus was born on 8 December 65 BC in Venusia in southern Italy, the son of an ex-slave as he tells us in his poems (e.g. *Satires* I.6.6), Rome was a republic governed by the Senate and People of Rome (SPQR). By the time he died fifty-seven years later in 8 BC the state was ruled by a single man, Augustus, and the republic had become a 'principate'. Power was moved from the hands of the senate and people to the court of the *princeps* who had gained his position by defeating the men who had in 44 BC murdered his adoptive father Julius Caesar, and then by defeating his rival Mark Antony at the battle of Actium in 31 BC. The poet went from being a total outsider whose appearance was not always *à la mode* (*Epistles* I.1.94–7) to being in effect the poet laureate who was asked to compose for the Secular Games in 17 BC, his personal change in position being a small reflection of the major changes at work in Roman politics of the time.

His father was clearly a man of some means with his own land and a job as a *coactor* (auctioneering manager); he was rich enough to send young Horace to be schooled in Rome and then to university in Athens, which is where he was in 44 BC when the news of Caesar's assassination broke. Horace joined up with the forces of Brutus, one of the leading assassins, and became a *tribunus militum* (senior officer). He fought for Brutus at the battle of Philippi in 42 BC where

the republicans were defeated. He returned to Rome and managed
to secure employment as a clerk to the treasury (*scriba quaestorius*),
which is somewhat surprising in view of his fighting on the wrong
side in the war against the man who was now the first emperor of
Rome and who could be a bad enemy. Horace was a friend of the
poet Virgil and through him was introduced to Maecenas – a close
associate of Octavian/Augustus (see below) – who became his patron.
Horace was introduced to Octavian himself and was even (it is said)
offered a job as a secretary with him – a job he refused. After some
time he obtained a small Sabine farm in the hills near Rome, probably
as a result of the patronage of Maecenas.

Horace began his career as a published poet with the first poem in
this book; the first book of *Satires* was published when he was about
thirty in 35 BC, followed by the *Epodes* and *Satires* II five years later in
30 BC. The *Epodes* and the *Satires* are forthright and at times outrageous
to modern ears in their views and in their language, but they all express
the spirit of frank outspokenness which was prized in the Roman
Republic and which we also see in the work of such republican poets as
Lucilius and Catullus. In general terms, the *Epodes* are invective poetry
attacking in a direct fashion the types of people around the poet such as
the fantasist who wants to live in the idyllic countryside but never quite
gets there in 2 or the aged woman who still wants her share of sex (12)
while the *Satires* are more restrained and less aggressive. In the 20s BC
he worked on the first three books of *Odes* which appeared in 23 BC. He
followed this with the first book of *Epistles* – a form of light didactic verse
purporting to be letters and containing philosophy and some satirical
content – mostly at his own expense. His most public commission was to
compose the *Carmen Saeculare* for the 'Secular Games' in 17 BC, which
was all part of the emperor Augustus' celebration of the national revival
under his rule. Horace composed a fourth book of *Odes* and some more
verse epistles – one of them addressed to the emperor personally. He
died in 8 BC, not long after the death of his patron Maecenas.

Maecenas

Poets throughout the ancient world were important people and there were many examples of political figures having a 'wise man' to offer advice and thought or to record their achievements: Scipio with his Laelius, for instance, Alexander with his Callisthenes, or Nero with his Seneca. The tradition whereby poetry was seen as an ethical force for good is as old as Homer himself – Agamemnon left a 'bard' with his wife Clytemnestra when he went to Troy in a (futile) bid to maintain her wifely fidelity (*Odyssey* III.267–8). Roman poets made something of a habit of dedicating their poems to men of action: Horace addresses *Satires* II.1 to the lawyer Trebatius, while Lucretius' patron was Memmius, and Tibullus' was Valerius Messalla Corvinus. Gaius Cilnius Maecenas was the man of power who was the patron of Horace and also Virgil, and it is hard to imagine the poetry of Horace being read or even written at all without him. Born around 69 BC into a rich family outside the senate (the 'equestrian order') he was proud of his Etruscan ancestry (something which Horace alludes to in the opening of *Satires* I.6 and *Odes* I.1). Like many a traditional wealthy *eques* ('knight' which denoted social rank rather than military status, as in the case of Cicero's rich friend Atticus) he never held any public office or entered the senate but found himself in a position of great influence at the court of the new emperor and from 40–20 BC seems to have exercised considerable sway over the younger Augustus, along with Augustus' military chief of staff, Agrippa. Horace gives us a wonderfully vivid description of his introduction to Maecenas in *Satire* I.6, and in I.5 he describes a journey to Brundisium made with the great man as part of a political diplomatic mission in 38 or 37 BC.

Patronage in the ancient world was a common phenomenon and seems to have determined the relationships between the great and the less exalted in many ways. In some cases it was financial – and Juvenal in his *Satires* gives a typically cynical account of the ways in which 'clients' were humiliated by their 'patrons' and how (equally) the clients would exploit the patrons for money at the morning 'greeting' (*salutatio*). The reality was not always so mercenary and in Horace's time it was a way in which mutual respect and benefit could be maintained (see OCD s.v. 'salutatio'). The financial side of Horace's friendship with Maecenas is usually seen as consisting of the 'Sabine estate' which the rich man gave to the poet (*Satires* II.6) and the poet at one point claims that he was driven to write by poverty (*Epistles* II.2.51–2). This is surely less than the whole truth. For one thing, writing poems did not pay a living wage then (any more than it usually does now); and for another, to obtain the position of what amounted to a senior civil servant (*scriba quaestorius*: for details see Fraenkel 2000: 14–15) he must have had some ready cash to buy the post. Nonetheless, the poet was given the generous gift of a Sabine estate and his relationship with his patron – and through him with Maecenas' own patron the emperor – clearly flourished and was of benefit to both sides.

Patronage of poets was, however, a tricky business. Alexander the Great made the mistake of commissioning the execrable Choerilus of Iasus to compose for him, and Horace mentions in his letter to Augustus the 'absurd poem' which rebounded to the discredit of the great man (*Epistles* II.1.232–8). A patron of poets had to have literary discernment, and this was where Maecenas also scored highly.

Maecenas was also astonishingly wealthy – probably as a result of the proscription of Octavian's opponents in 43 BC – and Horace mentions (*Satires* I.8.7, 14–15) his luxurious gardens. He was patron to many literary figures: Horace, Virgil, Varius and Propertius are the biggest names in his list but there were no doubt others. He has been seen in the past (not least by Syme) as a sort of Minister for Propaganda under the new regime, but this is a crude misapprehension both of the man and of the regime. For a much more nuanced and accurate account of the relationship between Horace and Maecenas see J. Griffin ('Caesar qui cogere posset: Augustus and the poets', in *Caesar Augustus: Seven Aspects* pp. 189–218), who eloquently puts it thus: 'The relationship with Maecenas could serve the poets as a smoked glass, as it were, between them and the naked glare of the sun of Augustus' (p. 195).

Roman sources paint quite a garish picture of Maecenas' Epicureanism and his Epicurean lifestyle. Seneca the Stoic (a philosophical school which was the chief rival to Epicureanism at the time and which preached a virtue of duty rather than pleasure) spends most of Letter 114 detailing the man's louche lifestyle as that of a decadent effeminate drunkard, with a prose style as loose as his morals. Syme (*The Roman Revolution* pp. 341–2) speculates about how Maecenas must have appeared to the 'dour' Agrippa – as a man 'who flaunted in public the luxury and the vices in which his tortured inconstant soul found refuge – silks, gems and the ambiguous charms of the actor Bathyllus: [Agrippa] despised the vile epicure who sought to introduce a novel delicacy to the banquets of Rome, the flesh of young donkeys.' His marriage to Terentia was stormy and for all his uxorious devotion (Seneca tells us that he would marry her every day) she rejected him daily and Seneca suggests that this caused his descent into drunkenness.

We have no way of knowing how exaggerated all this is. The man was certainly one of enormous power, and it is perhaps difficult to believe that so unstable a man would have held so much influence with the new emperor for so long, trusted to be the 'guardian of the city' during the war with Sextus Pompeius in 36 BC.

Satire

Satire is a peculiar genre. It tells its audience what the satirist thinks they need to hear and take note of, but it often does so with jeering mockery more in the manner of a stand-up comedian than that of a political speaker or an Old Testament prophet. Satire often seems to be urging its readers towards a life of sense and decency, decrying luxury and greed and appealing for old-style austerity of life and behaviour. Its targets are traditionally folly (where people are misguided in their choices), and vice (where they deliberately flout public morals), and much satire down the ages has been especially vicious in attacking the hypocrite who affects virtue while indulging his real vices in private. Satire speaks at some points like a journalist, lifting the lid on the nasty truths of human nature and society, while at other times it uses gentler humour in showing us 'Lord, what fools these mortals be!' It places itself with one foot in the camp of 'truth-telling' and another in the camp of 'entertainment', as famously epitomized in *Satires* I.1.24 where the poet says he is 'telling the truth with a smile' (*ridentem dicere verum*). It differs from comedy in that it is not solely seeking to amuse, although satire is often amusing: it differs from philosophy (which seeks to establish the truth for its own sake) by being an art-form which draws attention to itself and which seeks to entertain as well as to instruct, although some philosophers can be amusing as well as instructive. It is a hybrid and a mongrel, born of two very different parents, comedy and philosophy, and it is in many ways a parasitic genre in that it can latch on to other genres as the target for mockery of their forms of speech and attitudes (a form of satire known as 'parody'). It is also an encyclopaedic genre in that nothing is incapable of being included in its voluminous maw, from the vulgar details of life on the streets or in the bedroom to the finest reaches of religion and philosophy.

Satire is often self-consciously literary, but satire in verse is especially aware of its own status as an art-form and uses its poetry to mock poetry itself, debunking poetic affectation with its own brand of poetic parody but not above using poetic language to enhance the vividness of the scene being described. Parody of epic is easy for Latin verse satire as both epic and satire are composed in the hexameter metre and a subtle change of register of language is all it takes to show the lip of the poet curling in irony as he pronounces his verses. There are moments where the style of the lines hints that the speaker's rhetoric is itself the object of the satire (e.g. II.2.92–3) and it is always a moot point whether the *persona* of the speaker is the medium or the target of the satire, especially in places such as *Satire* II.2 where the poet claims to be reporting the ideas of another man.

Satire before Horace

satura quidem tota nostra est. 'Satire is entirely our own', said Quintilian (X.1.93) and it seems to have been a Roman recipe, even though it helped itself to some very Greek ingredients. The first author to compose *saturae* in Latin was Ennius (239–169 BC) who wrote plays and poetry as well as at least one prose work: what remains of his *Saturae* in six books is concerned with everyday life in Rome, and is composed in a variety of metres including some epic-sounding hexameters (e.g. fragments 3–4W, 23W) which admit of the possibility that he was sending up his own epic language such as we find in his historical epic the *Annales*. The next great figure in the history of Roman satire was Gaius Lucilius (180–102 BC); thirty books of his *Saturae* were composed in a variety of metres, showing a sharp line in wit and a caustic ability to attack his contemporaries. He attacked people by name and recounted his own sexual exploits; he denounced gluttony and political chicanery, and borrowed philosophical ideas while also mocking philosophical jargon.

ars est celare artem ('art consists in concealing the art'): Lucilius often reads as if he is improvising his lines but there is a good deal of conscious artistry at work in the ribald and raucous polemic, although Horace was later to call his work 'a muddy river from which

much should have been removed' (*Satires* I.4.11). He also presents
himself in a more or less ironic manner as the hero or anti-hero of
his own poetry, and thus introduces a very personal voice into the
poetic language.

Lucilius had fixed on the hexameter as the rhythm of satire by
his final book: but Varro (116–27 BC) who wrote voluminously on
matters of agriculture and language also produced 150 books of
'Menippean Satires' which are a blend of prose and verse, described
by Cicero (*Acad.* I.8) as 'a bit of philosophy with a dash of humour
and dialogue'. Their name and their inspiration was the Greek third-
century Cynic philosopher Menippus of Gadara – and the mixture of
prose and verse in satire was to be imitated a century later by Seneca
(in his *Apocolocyntosis*) and Petronius (in his *Satyricon*). The hybrid
satire using both prose and verse derived to some extent from the
Greek diatribe, a form of ethical 'sermon' delivered often by outdoor
speakers (see below on the 'The philosophical background' and see
also OCD s.v. 'diatribe').

Writing under the emperor Nero, the satirist Persius (AD 34–62)
composed only six satires, a meagre 650 lines in all, but took the
genre in a new direction with his application of Stoic philosophy as
the inspiration for his work. His poetry is involved and obscure but
deals with the stock themes – food, poetry, sex, power, gods – and
offers a more engaged and assertive model of satirical argument when
compared with the relaxed voice of Horace.

The last and the greatest of the Roman satirists was Juvenal (first
to second century AD) who wrote sixteen satires which took the
frankness of Lucilius and married it to the sharp wit of Horace and
Persius. Juvenal's savage indignation (in the earlier poems) and his
more philosophical reasoning (in the final two books of his *Satires*)
were all conveyed in elegant and highly stylized Latin which – like
Horace's poetry – nonetheless reads as a natural and spontaneous
outpouring of thoughts and feelings.

Horace's style of satire

Horace called his satirical poems *sermones* ('conversations') rather
than *saturae*. His is a gentler sort of satire in comparison to the
savagery of Lucilius, and Horace comes over as an ironic self-satirist
as much as a critic of other people. He famously tells (in the course
of I.5) of his hopes for sex with a servant-girl, only to be stood up
by her and end up 'staining his bedclothes', and his attempts to free
himself from a boring social climber in I.9 are a study in how good
manners can cause us grief. He links his mode of writing with the
ribald comedy of fifth century BC Athens (I.4) and he certainly speaks
frankly and crudely about sex (I.2) and food (II.2) in language worthy
of an Aristophanes, but he avoids overt political satire and so (for
instance) his account in I.5 of the journey to Brundisium – where
the fate of the world was to be decided with a treaty between Mark
Antony and Octavian – avoids all mention of the politics and only
writes about incidentals. His targets include hypocrisy and ambition,
and the set-piece descriptions of events such as the dinner party (II.8)
give us a vivid glimpse into the social world in which Horace, the
freedman's son, always (no doubt) felt himself to be something of an
outsider. He made good use of a variety of styles in his poems: parody
of epic, philosophical discourse in the manner of a didactic poet,
vivid raconteurish descriptions of Roman life, ribald humour (such
as the tale of Priapus and the witches in I.8) and even animal fables
such as the famous town mouse and country mouse (II.6).

The poems in this book are all excerpts from longer poems,
and they are also all single items in collections of poems published
together. Book 1 contains ten poems, of which the first three are
'diatribe' poems addressing ethical and moral issues, whereas the
others in the book are less didactic, being discussions of literary
aims (I.4, I.10), autobiographical accounts of the poet's life (I.5, I.6,
I.9) and comic flights of fancy (I.7, I.8). Book II returns to literary

manifesto matters in poem 1 and the reasons to write satire rather than epic. The other seven poems in the book deal with the dinner party both good (II.2, II.4) and awful (II.8), the Stoic philosophy of wisdom (II.3, II.7), the superiority of country living (II.6) and a burlesque of the underworld scene in book XI of Homer's *Odyssey* which treats of the Roman practice of legacy-hunting. Common satirical themes emerge from the eighteen poems: the mockery of folly and vice in the form of social climbing as opposed to genuine friendship, monetary greed and legacy-hunting, the recommendation of simple country life rather than the stressful luxury of the city, false wisdom as against common sense and following nature rather than fighting it, and the need for a sense of humour to face the serious side of life.

The poems are of course literary creations which are the fruit of careful composition, and they are fully aware of their place in the literary tradition of comedy, satire and philosophy. They are crafted with skill, especially when they seem to be simply the recording of a conversation between the poet and his audience on and off the page. His choice of the word *sermones* ('conversations') as the generic title of the poems is thus ironically modest and also revealing, as it suggests on the one hand the 'diatribe' (see above) of the Cynics and on the other hand the dialogues of Plato, both of which were concerned to explore issues of truth and moral common sense. This moves his satirical stance away from a mere assault on the behaviour of others towards the positive promotion of happiness. It also allows for the sort of teasing banter and humorous language which ancient philosophical writers such as Bion and Epicurus showed in their works, as we shall see in the next section.

The philosophical background

Ancient philosophy usually aspired to be practical and useful to its readers. Aristotle, for instance, in the *Nicomachean Ethics* gives us a guide to *eudaimonia* ('flourishing' or 'happiness') rather than simply abstruse logic-chopping, and he takes time to discuss those practical areas of life where moral choices need to be made. Horace's *Satires* similarly concern themselves above all with real life and make some use of the ideas of more than one major philosophical school and it is worth describing here something of the flavour of the schools of the Stoics, the Cynics and the Epicureans.

The Stoics (founded by Zeno of Citium (335–263 BC)) preached a philosophy whereby only virtue leads to happiness, only the wise can be virtuous and so only the virtuous man is wise. Virtue/duty alone matters and we should beware of letting our passions or emotions distract us from what reason tells us is the correct way to live. Virtue is shown in the ability to forgo selfish pleasures in the interest of the community and there were eminent Stoics who committed suicide as a model for the free man's final freedom to practise virtue – such as Cato when the victory of the dictator Caesar at Thapsus in April 46 BC told him that his free republic was now dead (see OCD s.v. 'Porcius Cato'(2)) This branch of philosophy recommends duty to the state and refuses to allow 'passions' (such as desire or fear) to stop the wise man exercising his reason in making moral choices.

Over against this high-minded elevation of duty over inclination are the schools of the Cynics and the Epicureans. The Cynics were founded by Diogenes (412–321 BC) who famously scorned the trappings of society and culture and lived in a barrel in the manner of a dog (*kynikos* in Greek means 'like a dog'), preaching that we are merely animals in clothes and can only be wise and happy when we live according to our animal natures. One of his later adherents, Bion of Borysthenes (see OCD s.v. Bion (1)), composed public speeches ('diatribes') on the same themes and these were a huge influence on Horace's early *Satires*. The diatribe was an ethical 'sermon' of popular philosophy delivered in the manner of a travelling speaker and which sought to make people think and change their ways, conveyed in a tone of hectoring banter directed at vice and folly and couched in vivid and aggressive imagery. Bion rejected the pretensions of the human mind and of society – and Roman satire certainly has more than a whiff of the Cynic (and the cynic) about it. The term 'diatribe' is close in meaning to the Latin term *sermo*, and the satirist's mocking tone of practical wisdom is very much in line with the style of Bion.

A more sophisticated version of cynicism is that of Epicurus (341–270 BC) who argued that we in fact seek pleasure and that goodness consists in what is likely to maximize pleasure over pain rather than the Stoic calculus of duty over inclination. The Epicureans did not, however, live a hedonistic lifestyle of orgies and banquets – they rather preached the wisdom of *parvum quod satis est* ('the little that is enough') and promoted an apolitical withdrawal from the world with the aim to 'live unnoticed' (cf. *Epistles* I.17.9–10). Epicurus believed that pleasure was primarily the cessation of pain and that accordingly once the pain had been stopped then the pleasure could not be increased: see, for instance, *Satire* I.1.45–60 for this argument as applied to money. Food, when we are hungry, gives pleasure in proportion to our need of it, but excess of food will only bring further pain (see *Satires* II.2.17–22). Nor does it matter what sort of food is provided so long as the hunger is stopped, and so the quest for *haute cuisine* is a waste of time. Epicurus himself was content with very little, and this elevation of the *parvum quod satis est* or *vivere parvo* becomes a key phrase in Roman Epicurean thought (cf. e.g. Horace *Satires* II.2.1, *Odes* III.16.43–4, Lucretius II.20–36) and the 'anything will do' argument is applied memorably to drink, food and sex in Horace (*Satires* I.2.111–19). For Epicureans the ideal residence was a garden rather than the crowded Forum and (like the Cynics) they argued that we can only be happy when we fully accept the truth of the world which included the finality of death and the atomic nature of the universe. The advice to restrict our appetites and so be content with what is readily available is one which Horace repeats many times in his poetry (e.g. *Odes* III.16.37–44). The early *Satires* show a very earthy Epicurean attitude towards sex (*Satires* I.2.114–19), money (I.1) and towards friendship, which Epicurus regarded as a moral virtue of great importance (I.3). Epicurus' attitude towards politics was very different from the *engagé* Stoics. On the one hand the wise Epicurean must avoid political ambition and the blind pursuit of power for the sake of a transient reputation: Lucretius demythologizes the sinner Sisyphus (doomed to push a boulder up a hill for all eternity) as the symbol of the man driven by political ambition (III.995–1002: cf. also Lucretius III.59–64). On the other hand, the wise man will be quite content to live in a state ruled by a monarch who lets him get on with his philosophizing in peace: as Oscar Wilde is reputed to have said, the trouble with Socialism is that it takes too many evenings.

Horace may have jokingly called himself 'a pig from the herd of Epicurus' (*Epistles* I.4.15–16) but he states that he did not 'sign up' to any of these schools – he described himself as *nullius addictus iurare in verba magistri* ('bound to swear allegiance to no master', *Epistles* I.1.14). That said, it is impossible to read Horace without meeting ideas and attitudes which can be traced back to those of the philosophical schools which provided much of the ethical thinking of the day.

The metre

Latin poetry is written in a fairly rigid system of metres, all of which in turn rely on the 'quantity' of each vowel as being either heavy/long or light/short, a long vowel being reckoned to take twice as long to pronounce as a short vowel. A syllable is reckoned to be a single vowel sound, followed either by nothing (an 'open' syllable) or by a consonant (a 'closed' syllable): usually a single consonant following a vowel is reckoned to be the first consonant of the following syllable (e.g. *ca-li-gi-ne*) and does not affect the length of the vowel: but where two or more consonants follow a vowel, the first one is included in the first syllable (*men-sa*) which is thus 'closed' and becomes lengthened – the exceptions being combinations of mute and liquid consonants (*b, c, g, p, t* followed by *r*, and *c, p, t*, followed by *l*) where both letters are considered as belonging to the following syllable (*ma-tris*) and need not lengthen the vowel. Diphthongs (*ae, eu, au*, etc.) are always long by nature: single vowels may be long or short by nature and may vary with inflection (e.g. the final *-a* of *mensa* is long by nature in the ablative case, short in the nominative) or they may be lengthened by position when followed by two or more consonants as indicated above (e.g. I.1.3 where the (short) final *-us* of *contentus* is followed by *v-* and so lengthened). In cases where a word ending with a vowel (or a vowel + *m* such as *iustam*) is followed by a word beginning with a vowel or *h*, the two syllables usually merge ('elide') into a single syllable, as at I.1.59 where the eight apparent syllables of *tantuli eget quanto est* are scanned as *tāntŭl(i) ĕg/ēt quānt/(o) ēst* (six syllables). Satiric hexameters tolerate some quite extreme elision: *quam aut* scanned as *qu'aut* in I.3.27 for instance, or the elision of *homo: illi* into *hom'illi* despite the punctuation in I.3.57. There are also cases where the poet does not elide but leaves the hiatus (which is where consecutive vowels are pronounced separately and not elided together) between the vowels, as at II.2.28 (*nŭm ădest*).

— means a long syllable

U means a short syllable

x means a syllable which may be either long or short

// means the caesura (word-end in the middle of a foot of a hexameter).

The hexameter is the 'epic' metre used by Homer and all later epic and didactic poets: it also became (after Lucilius) the metre of Latin verse satire. The line is divided into six 'feet', each of which is either a dactyl (a long syllable followed by two short syllables (—UU in conventional notation)) or a spondee (two long syllables (— —)). The last foot is always dissyllabic, and the last syllable of all may be either long or short. The metrical analysis of a line is called 'scansion' and a typical hexameter line (II.2.1) may be scanned thus:

— —/ — —/—∪∪/—// —/ —∪∪/— —
quāe vīr/tūs ēt /quāntă, bŏ/nī,// sīt/ vīvĕrĕ/ pārvō

where the // sign shows the 'caesura' – the word-break in the middle of a foot – which occurs in the third foot or (as here) the fourth: note how there is a mild caesura between the two short syllables of the dactyl in the third foot, followed by a further caesura in the fourth.

Hexameter verse thus had a stress or 'ictus' on the first syllable of each foot, somewhat like the downbeat in a bar of music. Latin also had a stress 'accent', whereby most words were stressed on the penultimate syllable, or on the antepenultimate if the penultimate were a short vowel. Thus the first line of *Satire* I.1 would be spoken:

quí fít, Maecénas, út némo, quám síbi sórtem

but 'scanned' metrically as:

quí fit/, Máecen/ás, ut /némo,/ quám sibi /sórtem

A better example of the clash of ictus and accent would be I.1.6, pronounced thus:

cóntra mercátor, návem iactántibus Aústris

but scanned thus:

cóntra /mérca/tór, nav/ém iac/tántibus Aústris

Quite how the two ways of reading Latin verse blended or competed is unclear: in epic hexameters there is a tendency for the stress accent and the metrical ictus to collide in the earlier and middle parts of the line but to coincide at the end, a tendency which is, however, abruptly broken when the line ends with a monosyllable as at I.1.48, 62, I.3.32, 56.

One strength of the hexameter is its versatility in the variation of quick and slow rhythms and also its readiness to vary the ending of the phrases and resist the urge to end the phrase with the ending of the line – a device known as 'enjambement'. To see some of this in action look at the well-turned lines (II.2.95–9) describing the fate of the big spender:

> *grandes rhombi patinaeque*
> *grande ferunt una cum damno dedecus: adde*
> *iratum patruum, vicinos, te tibi iniquum*
> *et frustra mortis cupidum, cum deerit egenti*
> *as, laquei pretium.*
> (massive turbots and dishes bring massive shame along with the financial ruin; throw in the angry uncle, neighbours and your own self-enmity, as you long in vain for death but are too poor to manage the penny which is the price of a noose.)

The opening phrase has pleasing anaphora (*grandes ... grande*) with the second instance promoted to the start of the line, leaving its referent (*dedecus*) for a few words to raise suspense and also create the punchy alliterative *damno dedecus*. The poet as teacher tells us (*adde*) to throw in the list of enemies (in asyndeton), culminating in the surprising fact that the big spender ends up his own worst enemy (*te tibi iniquum*). That would have sufficed, but the poet takes it a step further with the suicidal longing for death foiled by the man's sudden poverty (*egenti*): surprising perhaps in the case of a lavish spender of cash, but this one has spent it all and not even left himself enough to buy a noose with which to hang himself. The man's total lack of cash and the sick joke are accented by the monosyllable *as* placed in enjambement at the start of the line followed by the explanatory gloss *laquei pretium*.

Further reading

The literature on Horace is vast and this is a small selection of some books which students may find helpful in exploring the works of this poet.

Translations of the *Satires* include:

Horace (2011), *Satires and Epistles* (Oxford World's Classics), trans. J. Davie, Oxford: Oxford University Press.

Horace and Persius (2005), *The Satires of Horace and Persius* (Penguin Classics), trans. N. Rudd, London: Penguin Books.

Horace (1989), *Satires, Epistles, Ars Poetica*, (Loeb Classical Library), trans. H.R. Fairclough, Cambridge, MA: Harvard University Press, with facing Latin text, rev. edn.

Editions of the *Satires* include:

Gowers, E. (2012), *Horace Satires* (Cambridge Greek and Latin Classics) Book I, Cambridge: Cambridge University Press.

Brown, P.M. (1993), *Horace Satires* I, Warminster: Aris and Phillips.

Muecke, F. (1993), *Horace Satires* II, Warminster: Aris and Phillips.

Palmer, A. (1955), *Horace: Satires*, London: Macmillan.

General works on Horace:

Fraenkel, E. ([1957] 2000), *Horace*, Oxford: Oxford University Press, new edn.

Griffin, J. (1984), 'Augustus and the Poets: "Caesar qui cogere posset"', in F. Millar and E. Segal (eds), *Caesar Augustus: Seven Aspects*, Oxford: Oxford University Press.

Harrison, S., ed (2007), *The Cambridge Companion to Horace*, Cambridge: Cambridge University Press.

Hills, P. (2005), *Horace*, London: Bloomsbury.

West, D. (1967), *Reading Horace*, Edinburgh: Edinburgh University Press.

On Roman satire see especially:

Braund, S.H. (1989), *Satire and Society in Ancient Rome*, Exeter: University of Exeter Press.

Braund, S.H. (2013), *The Roman Satirists and their Masks*, Bristol: Bristol Classical Press.

Coffey, M. (1976), *Roman Satire*, London: Methuen.

Ferris-Hill, J.L. (2015), *Roman Satire and the Old Comic Tradition*, Cambridge: Cambridge University Press.

Freudenburg, K. (2001), *Satires of Rome*, Cambridge: Cambridge University Press.

Freudenburg, K. (2005), *The Cambridge Companion to Roman Satire*, Cambridge: Cambridge University Press.

Plaza, M. (2006), *The Function of Humour in Roman Verse Satire*, Oxford: Oxford University Press.

Rosen, R.M. (2007), *Making Mockery: the Poetics of Ancient Satire*, Oxford: Oxford University Press.

Rudd, N. (1998), *Themes in Roman Satire*, Bristol: Bristol Classical Press.

Sullivan, J.P., ed (1963), *Critical Essays on Roman Literature: Satire*, London: Routledge.

On Horace's *Satires* see especially:

Freudenburg, K., ed. (2009), *Horace: Satires and Epistles* (Oxford Readings in Classical Studies), Oxford: Oxford University Press.

Rudd, N. (1994), *The Satires of Horace*, Bristol: Bristol Classical Press.

On the use of metre see:

Morgan, L. (2010), *Musa Pedestris – Metre and Meaning in Roman Verse*, Oxford: Oxford University Press.

Raven, D.S. (2010), *Latin Metre*, London: Bloomsbury, new edn.

Useful books on Latin grammar used in this edition include:

Allen, J.H. and J.B. Greenough (2006), *New Latin Grammar*, New York: Dover Publications, referred to in the commentary as AG.

Morwood, J. (1999), *Latin Grammar*, Oxford: Oxford University Press.

For more information on all things ancient see:

The Oxford Classical Dictionary (OCD).

The best Latin dictionary available in English is:

The Oxford Latin Dictionary (OLD).

Text

I.1

qui fit, Maecenas, ut nemo, quam sibi sortem
seu ratio dederit seu fors obiecerit, illa
contentus vivat, laudet diversa sequentes?
'o fortunati mercatores!' gravis annis
miles ait, multo iam fractus membra labore.   5
contra mercator, navem iactantibus Austris,
'militia est potior. quid enim? concurritur: horae
momento cita mors venit aut victoria laeta.'
agricolam laudat iuris legumque peritus,
sub galli cantum consultor ubi ostia pulsat.   10
ille, datis vadibus qui rure extractus in urbem est,
solos felices viventes clamat in urbe.

*13–27: If God were to let them change their lives as they say they would like,
they would refuse, and God would be right to be angry with them. Horace
says that he is happy to use humour to make his points more palatable, like
teachers offering biscuits to pupils.*

ille gravem duro terram qui vertit aratro,
perfidus hic caupo, miles nautaeque per omne
audaces mare qui currunt, hac mente laborem   30
sese ferre, senes ut in otia tuta recedant,
aiunt, cum sibi sint congesta cibaria: sicut
parvula – nam exemplo est – magni formica laboris
ore trahit quodcumque potest atque addit acervo
quem struit, haud ignara ac non incauta futuri.   35

quae, simul inversum contristat Aquarius annum,
non usquam prorepit et illis utitur ante
quaesitis sapiens; cum te neque fervidus aestus
demoveat lucro, neque hiems, ignis, mare, ferrum,
nil obstet tibi dum ne sit te ditior alter. 40
quid iuvat immensum te argenti pondus et auri
furtim defossa timidum deponere terra?
'quod si comminuas vilem redigatur ad assem.'
at ni id fit, quid habet pulchri constructus acervus?
milia frumenti tua triverit area centum, 45
non tuus hoc capiet venter plus ac meus: ut si
reticulum panis venales inter onusto
forte vehas umero, nihilo plus accipias quam
qui nil portarit. vel dic quid referat intra
naturae fines viventi, iugera centum an 50
mille aret? 'at suave est ex magno tollere acervo.'
dum ex parvo nobis tantundem haurire relinquas,
cur tua plus laudes cumeris granaria nostris?
ut tibi si sit opus liquidi non amplius urna
vel cyatho, et dicas 'magno de flumine mallem 55
quam ex hoc fonticulo tantundem sumere.' eo fit
plenior ut si quos delectet copia iusto,
cum ripa simul avulsos ferat Aufidus acer.
at qui tantuli eget quanto est opus, is neque limo
turbatam haurit aquam, neque vitam amittit in undis. 60
at bona pars hominum decepta cupidine falso
'nil satis est' inquit, 'quia tanti quantum habeas sis.'
quid facias illi? iubeas miserum esse, libenter
quatenus id facit: ut quidam memoratur Athenis
sordidus ac dives, populi contemnere voces 65
sic solitus: 'populus me sibilat; at mihi plaudo
ipse domi, simul ac nummos contemplor in arca.'
Tantalus a labris sitiens fugientia captat
flumina – quid rides? mutato nomine de te
fabula narratur; congestis undique saccis 70

indormis inhians et tamquam parcere sacris
cogeris aut pictis tamquam gaudere tabellis.
nescis quo valeat nummus, quem praebeat usum?
panis ematur, holus, vini sextarius, adde
quis humana sibi doleat natura negatis.   75
an vigilare metu exanimem, noctesque diesque
formidare malos fures, incendia, servos,
ne te compilent fugientes, hoc iuvat? horum
semper ego optarim pauperrimus esse bonorum.
'at si condoluit temptatum frigore corpus   80
aut alius casus lecto te adfixit, habes qui
adsideat, fomenta paret, medicum roget ut te
suscitet ac reddat gnatis carisque propinquis.'
non uxor salvum te vult, non filius; omnes
vicini oderunt, noti, pueri atque puellae.   85
miraris, cum tu argento post omnia ponas,
si nemo praestet quem non merearis amorem?
an si cognatos, nullo natura labore
quos tibi dat, retinere velis servareque amicos,
infelix operam perdas, ut si quis asellum   90
in Campo doceat parentem currere frenis?
denique sit finis quaerendi, cumque habeas plus,
pauperiem metuas minus, et finire laborem
incipias, parto quod avebas, ne facias quod
Ummidius quidam: non longa est fabula: dives   95
ut metiretur nummos: ita sordidus, ut se
non umquam servo melius vestiret; adusque
supremum tempus, ne se penuria victus
opprimeret metuebat. at hunc liberta securi
divisit medium, fortissima Tyndaridarum.   100

*101–21: Wasting money foolishly as a spendthrift is just as bad as being a
miser and the poet recommends moderation in all things and recapitulates
his earlier argument that discontentment with their status (both personal
and financial) makes people unhappy and unable to see the good things
they could enjoy.*

I.3

1–24: This poem begins with a comic sketch of the singer Tigellius as a man of infuriating extremes, and then attacks the tendency to be too indulgent with ourselves while criticizing other people.

cum tua pervideas oculis mala lippus inunctis,   25
cur in amicorum vitiis tam cernis acutum
quam aut aquila aut serpens Epidaurius? at tibi contra
evenit, inquirant vitia ut tua rursus et illi.
iracundior est paulo, minus aptus acutis
naribus horum hominum; rideri possit eo quod   30
rusticius tonso toga defluit et male laxus
in pede calceus haeret: at est bonus, ut melior vir
non alius quisquam, at tibi amicus, at ingenium ingens
inculto latet hoc sub corpore. denique te ipsum
concute num qua tibi vitiorum inseverit olim   35
natura aut etiam consuetudo mala; namque
neglectis urenda filix innascitur agris.
illuc praevertamur, amatorem quod amicae
turpia decipiunt caecum vitia, aut etiam ipsa haec
delectant, veluti Balbinum polypus Hagnae.   40
vellem in amicitia sic erraremus, et isti
errori nomen virtus posuisset honestum.
ac pater ut gnati sic nos debemus amici
si quod sit vitium non fastidire: strabonem
appellat paetum pater, et pullum, male parvus   45
si cui filius est, ut abortivus fuit olim
Sisyphus; hunc varum distortis cruribus, illum
balbutit scaurum pravis fultum male talis.
parcius hic vivit: frugi dicatur. ineptus
et iactantior hic paulo est: concinnus amicis   50
postulat ut videatur. at est truculentior atque
plus aequo liber: simplex fortisque habeatur.
caldior est: acres inter numeretur. opinor,

haec res et iungit iunctos et servat amicos.
at nos virtutes ipsas invertimus atque   55
sincerum cupimus vas incrustare. probus quis
nobiscum vivit, multum demissus homo: illi
tardo cognomen, pingui, damus. hic fugit omnes
insidias nullique malo latus obdit apertum,
cum genus hoc inter vitae versetur ubi acris   60
invidia atque vigent ubi crimina: pro bene sano
ac non incauto fictum astutumque vocamus.
simplicior quis et est qualem me saepe libenter
obtulerim tibi, Maecenas, ut forte legentem
aut tacitum impellat quovis sermone molestus: 65
'communi sensu plane caret' inquimus. eheu,
quam temere in nosmet legem sancimus iniquam!
nam vitiis nemo sine nascitur: optimus ille est
qui minimis urgetur. amicus dulcis ut aequum est
cum mea compenset vitiis bona, pluribus hisce –   70
si modo plura mihi bona sunt – inclinet, amari
si volet: hac lege in trutina ponetur eadem.
qui ne tuberibus propriis offendat amicum
postulat, ignoscet verrucis illius; aequum est
peccatis veniam poscentem reddere rursus.   75

76–133: The poem ends with an attack on the Stoic ideas of moral inflexibility: all offences are not equal and the rigid Stoic 'wise man' who thinks he is king is far less happy than the poet with his indulgent friends.

II.2

quae virtus et quanta, boni, sit vivere parvo
(nec meus hic sermo est, sed quae praecepit Ofellus
rusticus, abnormis sapiens crassaque Minerva)
discite, non inter lances mensasque nitentes,
cum stupet insanis acies fulgoribus et cum   5
acclinis falsis animus meliora recusat,
verum hic impransi mecum disquirite. 'cur hoc?'
dicam si potero. male verum examinat omnis
corruptus iudex. leporem sectatus equove
lassus ab indomito – vel si Romana fatigat   10
militia adsuetum graecari, seu pila velox
molliter austerum studio fallente laborem,
seu te discus agit, pete cedentem aera disco –
cum labor extuderit fastidia, siccus, inanis
sperne cibum vilem: nisi Hymetia mella Falerno   15
ne biberis diluta. foris est promus et atrum
defendens pisces hiemat mare: cum sale panis
latrantem stomachum bene leniet. unde putas aut
qui partum? non in caro nidore voluptas
summa sed in te ipso est. tu pulmentaria quaere   20
sudando; pinguem vitiis albumque neque ostrea
nec scarus aut poterit peregrina iuvare lagois.
vix tamen eripiam posito pavone velis quin
hoc potius quam gallina tergere palatum,
corruptus vanis rerum, quia veneat auro   25
rara avis et picta pandat spectacula cauda;
tamquam ad rem attineat quicquam. num vesceris ista
quam laudas pluma? cocto num adest honor idem?
carne tamen quamvis distat nil, hac magis illam
imparibus formis deceptum te petere! esto: 30

31-69: The poet continues his criticism of the quest for luxury in dining and then turns to the opposite vice to gluttony, that is, meanness and living on scraps, which he also condemns.

accipe nunc victus tenuis quae quantaque secum 70
adferat. imprimis valeas bene: nam variae res
ut noceant homini credas, memor illius escae
quae simplex olim tibi sederit; at simul assis
miscueris elixa, simul conchylia turdis,
dulcia se in bilem vertent stomachoque tumultum 75
lenta feret pituita. vides ut pallidus omnis
cena desurgat dubia? quin corpus onustum
hesternis vitiis animum quoque praegravat una,
atque adfigit humo divinae particulam aurae.
alter ubi dicto citius curata sopori 80
membra dedit vegetus praescripta ad munia surgit.
hic tamen ad melius poterit transcurrere quondam,
sive diem festum rediens advexerit annus,
seu recreare volet tenuatum corpus, ubique
accedent anni et tractari mollius aetas 85
imbecilla volet: tibi quidnam accedet ad istam
quam puer et validus praesumis mollitiem, seu
dura valetudo inciderit seu tarda senectus?
rancidum aprum antiqui laudabant, non quia nasus
illis nullus erat, sed, credo, hac mente, quod hospes 90
tardius adveniens vitiatum commodius quam
integrum edax dominus consumeret. hos utinam inter
heroas natum tellus me prima tulisset!
das aliquid famae, quae carmine gratior aurem
occupet humanam: grandes rhombi patinaeque 95
grande ferunt una cum damno dedecus: adde
iratum patruum, vicinos, te tibi iniquum
et frustra mortis cupidum, cum deerit egenti
as, laquei pretium. 'iure' inquit 'Trausius istis
iurgatur verbis; ego vectigalia magna 100
divitiasque habeo tribus amplas regibus.' ergo
quod superat non est melius quo insumere possis?
cur eget indignus quisquam, te divite? quare
templa ruunt antiqua deum? cur, improbe, carae

non aliquid patriae tanto emetiris acervo?   105
uni nimirum recte tibi semper erunt res.
o magnus posthac inimicis risus! uterne
ad casus dubios fidet sibi certius? hic qui
pluribus adsuerit mentem corpusque superbum,
an qui contentus parvo metuensque futuri   110
in pace ut sapiens aptarit idonea bello?

112–36: The poem concludes with an image of the contented countryman Ofellus practising what he preaches: it ends with a fine philosophical conclusion on the unreliability of fortune. We cannot hold on to anything for very long, and property always changes hands. 'Live brave lives and hold out brave hearts against adversity' is the final sentiment.

Commentary Notes

I.1

This is a very effective opening poem to the book. It bursts into life without any introduction (as a 'conversation' (*sermo*) would) and it sets the moral points within vividly drawn vignettes of life in the ancient world, complete with dodgy innkeepers (29), traders plying the seas for profit (29–30), the busy ant (33–8), the miser hissing at the people around him as he gazes on his treasure (66–7), teachers bribing their pupils with biscuits (25–6) and the sick man paying for care (80–3). It brings in Greek mythology (68–70, 100) and named individuals familiar from literature as well as from life (101–2, 120). The poet dramatizes his arguments by letting the other side speak: setting up a straw man in this way gives Horace the chance to articulate the objections and then to shred them to bits in a lively jocular fashion.

The two topics covered are those of 'discontent with one's lot in life' and 'avarice', both familiar targets of Roman satire from Lucilius to Juvenal, and Horace cleverly draws the two together at the end by letting the reader see that these are two aspects of the same deeper problem of discontentment and anxiety. Feeling that the grass is greener on the other side of the fence and working furiously to pile up money are both symptoms of an insecurity which never lets a person rest or be truly happy. The poem thus also introduces the style of satire which Horace espouses – mockery in a positive spirit of helping us to be happier individuals, didactic but not simply high-handed preaching, benevolent rather than scornful – except of the wasted lives lived in pursuit of the wrong ends.

Summary of the poem

Why are people so discontented and so envious of others? (1–22) A secure retirement is what people say they work for, like the ant who builds up a winter store when the sun shines (23–38) but at least the ant enjoys its store, whereas the compulsive money-grabber can never have enough (39–100). Not that the poet endorses prodigal living either (101–7), and the poet returns at the end (108–21) to the overarching theme of contentment which is the central theme of the poem and the essential ingredient of a happy life.

1 Maecenas is personally named in the opening sentence as the poet's patron, just as he is in the opening of the *Odes*, the *Epodes* and the *Epistles*, and as Virgil (another of his clients) addresses him in the opening of the *Georgics* (I.1–2). For Maecenas' life and influence, see the Introduction.

1–3 qui is here a question word meaning 'how' and the phrase **qui fit … ut** has the sense 'how does it happen that nobody …', with the **ut** + subjunctive as a form of consecutive clause. The **sortem** which is placed in the relative clause is picked up by **illa**: 'how does it happen that nobody lives content with the lot (**sortem**) which either choice … or chance … but rather [each man] praises those people who …?' The poet bursts into speech directed at the patron without any preamble, as he later (I.3.64–5) tells us is his habit, and Maecenas does not reply.

2 There is a nice contrast between events which are 'given' (**dederit**) by **ratio** (rational choice) and those which are 'thrown at us' (**obiecerit**) by random chance (**fors**).

3 The two verbs are juxtaposed neatly but we have to understand *sed quisque* between them: 'nobody lives content ... (but rather each man) praises people who pursue different ends.' Contentment is the goal of Horace's philosophical life and one which his father taught him (*Satires* I.4.108).

4-12 Horace illustrates his general point with several examples drawn from different walks of life but all sharing the same feeling of discontent with their lot in life. Notice how the poet dramatizes the issue with the use of quoted speech (4, 7–8), the thumbnail sketching of the speaker's age and character (4–5), the use of the ablative absolute to locate the **mercator** in a time and place (6), the contrast of the pompously phrased **iuris legumque peritus** over against the simple **agricolam** (9) and the irony in 10.

4-5 Soldiers expected to be allowed to retire after completing a specified term of service – and certainly by the age of forty-five, although Tacitus (*Annals* I.34) tells us that they could serve in the ranks for many years and that in AD 14 they mutinied over this issue, showing Germanicus their *curvata senio membra* ('limbs bent with old age') and their toothless gums as proof of their long service. Horace makes the point twice here, both in the brief **gravis annis** ('heavy with years') and then in the more specific **multo iam fractus membra labore** where **membra** is an accusative of respect ('broken as to his limbs').

6 The merchant sailor is himself at the mercy of the winds which are 'tossing' his ship, and the spondees of the first four feet of the line indicate the time dragging as the hapless sailor fears for his life. For the terror inspired by storms at sea for the mariner see Juvenal *Satire* XII.30–82. The verb **ait** has to be supplied from line 5.

7-8 The merchant's idealized view of military service is based on his own experience of long sea-storms as contrasted with the assumed

brevity of a battle. The rapid recourse to action is brought out first
of all in the style of the one-word impersonal passive **concurritur**
('battle is joined') and then explained in the categorical opposition of
'swift death' or 'joyful victory' (in a neat chiasmus) both attainable in
'the crisis of an hour', where the crisis of life or death is hung over the
line-end in a teasing enjambement.

9–10 The **iuris legumque peritus** is given a grand title to suit his
important role as an 'expert' in legal matters, and the following line
details the intrusive banging of his door at dawn by somebody seeking
his advice (**consultor**). There is irony in the fact that even the country-
dwelling farmer would be allowed to sleep until the cock crows,
whereas the urban lawyer is not. **sub** here means 'just before'. Note the
way the line/sentence ends with the emphatic verb **pulsat**, suggestive
of the 'battering' of the door, presumably to awaken those indoors; the
same verb is used of a nocturnal mugging at Juvenal III.289.

11–12 *vades dare* is to provide bail and we have to imagine the
country-dweller summoned to the city to take part in a legal matter:
he is 'dragged' (**extractus**) from the countryside (**rure**) presumably in
a matter not of his choosing, but then finds the city life so wonderful
that he positively shouts (**clamat**) his feelings. The similar endings
of two lines (**in urbem est ... in urbe**) and the string of accusative
plurals (**solos felices viventes**) all suggest the oafish manner in which
this rustic speaks. The superficial attraction of city-living will be
explored and dismissed in great detail in the story of the town mouse
and the country mouse in II.6.79–117.

*13–27: The poet tells us that if God were to allow them to change their
lives as they profess to wish, they would refuse, and God would be
right to be angry with them. Horace then tells us that he is happy to
use humour to make his points more palatable, like teachers offering
biscuits to pupils.*

28-107 After the opening section on discontent with our lot in life, Horace now turns to what will be the major concern of the poem – money and our attitude towards it.

28-30 Four categories of 'worker' are described, with emphasis on the labour required of three of them and a hint at the avarice which they are going to exemplify.

28 Horace does not specify 'farmer' but the grand epic line is more than enough both to identify the worker and to create an image of his toil. The land is 'heavy' and the plough is 'hard', and the spondaic rhythm of **-em duro terram qui** is expressive of the labour involved – a very different view of agriculture from the idyllic view found in Virgil *Georgics* II.459-60 and in Horace *Epodes* II. There are no short-cuts available for this farmer.

29-30 The innkeeper (**caupo**) was often (cf. I.5.4) seen as a crook, notorious for (e.g.) watering down the drink and on occasion even for murder and robbery (cf. the famous tale told by Cicero *de Divinatione* I.57). Horace neatly juxtaposes the three categories of men together to suggest that they are united in a single goal and the enthusiasm of the soldier and the sailor to travel is enhanced by the details of 'every one' (**omne**) of the seas and the strong verb **currunt** (metaphorical here (as at *Epistles* I.11.27) but suggestive of the unnatural effort involved), coupled with the adjective **audaces** ('reckless').

30 hac mente here means 'with this purpose'.

31-40 aiunt ('they say') is the main verb and their protestations of prudential forward planning ('so that when they are old men they may retire into safe leisure') are put into ironic indirect statement – ironic, as the poet is later (38-40) going to cast doubt on the sanity of this apparently sound reasoning. The extended positive image of

the ant (32–5) is part of the argument being put forward here; the
poet neatly breaks in with his objections at line 36 carrying on the
description but leading to the telling and damning difference in 38
(**cum te …**). The language used of the miser is heavily didactic with
a clumsy parenthesis (**nam exemplo est**) and epic and rhetorical
features designed to characterize the sententious man: a register which
the poet breaks with his more personal and peremptory interrogation
(**te … te**) couched in impatient asyndeton (39) and monosyllabic
finger-jabbing (**nil … dum ne sit te**).

32 The imagery of **congesta cibaria** is that of 'heaped-up rations' and
looks forward to the analogy of the ant which follows.

33–8 The ant was renowned for its Stakhanovite work ethic and its
prudential hoarding of food: see, for example, Aesop's fable (Perry
373) where the busy wise ant who uses the good weather to build up
supplies for the winter (see lines 36–7 and cf. Virgil *Georgics* I.186
('the ant anxious for its destitute old age') and *Aeneid* IV.403) is
contrasted with the imprudent grasshopper who spends the sunny
days singing and then grovels to the ant for food in winter.

33 There is a nice oxymoron of the 'smaller than small' (**parvula** is a
diminutive of *parva*) ant and its 'massive' (**magni**) labour. **exemplo**
is a predicative dative (Morwood pp. 12–13) – it is to 'serve as an
example' while **magni … laboris** is a genitive of quality (Morwood
p. 8), giving the phrase an epic ring.

34 The ability of the ant to carry food with its mouth was mentioned by
other poets (e.g. Ovid *Ars Amatoria* I.94). The point of **quodcumque
potest** is that it carries as much as it can – rather as the sailor goes
over *all* the seas. The phrase continues the self-justification of the
avaricious man.

35 haud ignara ac non incauta futuri is a lavish rhetorical expression (cf. Virgil *Aeneid* IV.508) expressive of the self-justification at work here. Note the double litotes of 'not unaware and not without thought for'.

36 The arrival of winter is well conveyed with the naming of the constellation **Aquarius** (which the sun enters on 16 January), the powerful verb **contristat** (literally 'saddens') and the participial phrase **inversum ... annum** denoting the year 'turned inside out' from the sunny summer to the dreary winter. **quae** is a connecting relative with strong adversative force ('but he ...'), showing that the ant is very different from the miser as the ant at least enjoys his store of goods.

37-8 prorepit is the exact word for the ant who does not 'creep out' – and the plentiful supply of food is well brought out by the enjambement of **ante / quaesitis** where **ante** is adverbial ('earlier') and the non-specific nature of 'what has been sought out' (**quaesitis**).

38 The sentence rounds off with the summarizing adjective **sapiens** – the ant is 'wise', just as anybody who saves for the future is wise. If the miser thinks he is thus justified, he is mistaken, as the following lines show.

38-40 The key difference is that the ant works in summer and then enjoys the fruits of his labour in the winter; the miser never stops working and so never gets the benefit of his toil. The ant is sensible in making provision for lean times – whereas the miser is just determined to be the richest man in town.

38 cum here means something like 'but since' and governs both **demoveat** (39) and **obstet** (40) in asyndeton. **te** does not refer to

Maecenas, but rather the miser whose behaviour is under discussion.
It is striking that the poet now addresses this man in the second
person, turning the general remarks into a vitriolic attack and raising
the temperature of the satiric aggression, allowing the poem to launch
into a dialogue with imagined objections from the miser in lines 43,
51, 55–6, 62, 65–6, 80–3, 101–2.

38–9 The list of things which would prevent the normal person from
working begins with the 'boiling' heat of summer (**fervidus aestus**) and
then jumps to winter (**hiems**) when the ant stayed at home, followed
by a breathless list in asyndeton of the epic foes of 'fire, sea, sword'.
This is hyperbolic cliché – see OLD s.v. *ferrum* 5c for many examples
of this sort of phrase in prose writers – broken up by the insertion of
mare (water cancelling out **ignis** and recalling line 30) which makes
the sequence more effective as a jumble of very different but equally
plausible things which would jeopardize the quest for money. The
miser refuses to budge (nothing would **demoveat** him) and is set on
removing any obstacle (**obstet** 40) to his supreme wealth. The short
phrase **nil obstet** (40) is a neat summary of the list of obstacles in 38–9
(**neque fervidus … mare, ferrum**).

40 dum ne … alter + subjunctive has here the sense of 'to make sure
that nobody else' and **ditior** is a compressed form of *divitior* ('richer').
For the thought cf. Juvenal X.23–5.

41–4 The argument can be reduced to: 'what is the good of money if it
is not used?' 'But if I use it, it will all go!' 'But if you don't use it what is
the point of having it?' Horace neatly begins to dramatize the conflict
in an imaginary dialogue (see 38n.).

41 quid iuvat ('what good does it do you to …?') takes an accusative
and infinitive. The qualifying terms **immensum … pondus** are placed

near **iuvat** to suggest that (for all) its immense size, the hoard will not give pleasure. **immensum** is from *in-metior* and so indicates 'too large to be measured': this and the singular term **pondus** indicate that the size of the holding reduces all the coins to a mere 'weight' of gold and silver (cf. 96 below).

42 There is a nice irony in the miser building up a fortune which makes him scared (**timidum**) and avoiding thieves by behaving like one himself – **furtim** literally means 'in the manner of a thief (*fur*)'.

43 The *as* was the smallest Roman coin and so was proverbially 'cheap' (**vilem**) so that **ad assem** meant 'down to one's last halfpenny' (*Epistles* II.2.27; see also *Satires* I.6.13, Catullus V.3, XXXIII.7).

44 ni id fit means 'if that does not happen' (i.e. if you do not make use of the money). **pulchri** is a partitive genitive ('what [amount of] beauty'). The line ends with a nice image of the **constructus acervus** almost as if the poet were quoting the miser's own evaluation of his 'pile'. The term **acervus** was also used (e.g. *Epistles* II.1.47, Cicero *de divinatione* II.11) to refer to the famous Greek paradox of the *sorites* ('how many grains does it take to make a heap? If I remove one grain it is still a heap, so it will never stop being a heap no matter how many individual grains I remove'). This is not an argument which will impress the miser who refuses to lose even one small part of his fortune, but the idea of 'grains' common in the argument's formulation leads neatly on to lines 45–6.

45–51 The poet moves to more Epicurean considerations. Epicurus argued that once bodily needs have been satisfied, pleasure cannot be increased but only varied (see, for example, Lucretius II.20–36). We are subject to the 'boundaries of Nature' (**naturae fines** line 50) and the wise man will choose to live within these if he is to be happy and to maximize his pleasure. Furthermore, some pleasures are necessary and natural (e.g. food and drink), others are natural but not necessary (e.g. sex), while the third category are neither natural nor necessary (luxuries).

45 We have to understand the partitive genitive plural *medimnum* ('bushels') after **milia … centum** ('100,000 bushels of grain'), and we also need to understand *si* with **triverit** which is the future perfect tense of *tero*. The verb's meaning is essentially 'thresh' but there is also a sense of 'wearing away' suggestive of the futility of the miser's behaviour.

46 The line uses a remarkably blunt register of language with seven monosyllables (including the colloquial **plus ac** for the more elevated *plus quam* in the sense 'more than') as the misguided calculations of the miser are reduced to what the human stomach can hold. For the use of the stomach to make a satirical point see V.7–8, Juvenal XI.38–41, Euripides *Cyclops* 335. **hoc** (ablative of cause) here means 'because of this', and **plus** is neuter accusative singular as the object of **capiet**. **ut si** means *velut si* ('just as if').

46–9 The poet continues the idea of grain/bread with the image of slaves walking as a gang with one of them carrying the bread bag but getting no more for doing so than the ones who carry nothing – a nice illustration from the other end of the social spectrum from 45–6. **venales inter** means *inter venales* ('amongst the slaves'). **si … forte** simply means 'if you happened to be the one who …'. **onusto** ('burdened' agreeing with **umero**) makes **vehas** clearer as involving a heavy burden and makes the dismal 'nothing greater' (**nihilo plus**) all the more disappointing, especially in comparison with the one who has carried the monosyllabic **nil**. The verbs **vehas** and **accipias** are both present subjunctive indicating a remote conditional in the future ('if you were to carry, you would …') while **portarit** is the contracted form of *portaverit* (perfect subjunctive relating to the man who 'has carried' nothing).

49–51 The Roman *iugerum* was about two-thirds of an acre and was the standard measurement of land. Horace neatly uses the term **fines** metaphorically (the 'boundaries of nature' – see 45–51n. above) and then moves on to literal measurements of land. *refert* is an impersonal verb ('it matters') and so the subjunctive phrase **quid referat** means 'what difference would it make?' and the dative participle **viventi** means 'to a man who lives', supplying also the subject ('if he ploughs') to the verb **aret**.

51–3 The miserly straw man speaks up again, to be refuted by the poet in strict logical terms with a *reductio ad absurdum*: if both men consume the same amount then the size of the **acervo** is immaterial, and a drink will be the same from a spring as from a river.

52 dum (+ subjunctive **relinquas**) here means 'provided that you allow me' and **haurire** has the sense of 'drawing off' as much as one needs (cf. 60 below) and is contrasted with **tollere** ('to remove') in the previous line. **tantundem** derives from *tantus* and allows the poet to take 'just as much' as (i.e. no less than) the miser (cf. 65). **parvo** understands **acervo** from the previous line and contrasts with **magno** there.

53 granaria are granaries able to feed hundreds while a *cumera* was a mere basket or box to hold perhaps a day's worth of corn; the respective hoards of the two men are juxtaposed for ironic comparison, with the added touch that the granaries belong to one man alone (**tua**) while the baskets are 'ours' (**nostris**) – a point developed below at 84–7. **laudes** is a deliberative subjunctive ('Why should you praise?') and the ablative **cumeris** is one of comparison ('more (**plus**) than …').

54–5 ut … si means 'it is as if …' as at 46. The construction *opus est* + dative + ablative means 'there is a need' with the person needing (**tibi**) in the dative and the thing(s) needed in the ablative – here the **urnā vel cyatho**, with **non amplius** almost parenthetic ('and no more'). The **urna** was an urn or vessel, while the **cyathus** was a ladle. The poet imagines the need for fluid – first of all just a single urnful and then (afterthought) reduces it to perhaps just a single ladleful, to enhance the contrast with the hyperbolic **magno de flumine**.

56 fonticulo is diminutive of *fons* and contrasts neatly with the great river of 55, while **tantundem sumere** parallels **tantundem haurire** in 52.

56–8 eo fit … ut: 'it gets to such a point that (**ut**) anyone who is pleased by a supply which is more plentiful than is right is torn away along with the riverbank and swept off by the fierce Aufidus.' The poet takes the analogy of the river and makes it all too literal with a put-down conclusion that the desire to 'drink from a great river' will see you swept off your feet. **iusto** is ablative of comparison after **plenior**, the two words framing the line. Note the effective juxtaposition of **avulsos ferat** denoting the two violent actions of the river in a short devastating phrase. The river **Aufidus** (now called the Ofanto) was the river of Horace's childhood in Venusia; his naming of it without explanation suggests that he is writing for people who know the area.

59–60 The poet concludes this point with a further consideration: water from a stream is clear whereas that from a violent river is muddy – and who wants to drink muddy water? – and streams are safe to wade into for water while a river will drown you in its current. **tantuli** ('just the tiny amount': in the genitive case after **eget**) is the diminutive of *tantus* which looks forward to the mythological **Tantalus** who will appear at 68. For the idea that the wise man will only want what he actually needs and no more see *Satires* II.2 *Odes* I.31.15–16, II.11.5, II.16.13, Cicero *Tusculan Disputations* V.89, Juvenal XIV.316–20. Line 60 is elegantly constructed with a strong break at the caesura and the terms for 'water' (**aquam … undis**) at the end of each half of the line with the verbs central in each phrase.

61 This is mathematically the central line in the poem and is suitable as a motto for the whole satire, mocking as it does the folly and the delusion behind the desires of most people (cf. Juvenal X.1–4: Horace thanks his Athenian education for sparing him such delusions at *Epistles* II.2.44).

62 tanti is genitive of value ('worth so much') and so the phrase means 'you are only worth what you possess' – with the key verbs juxtaposed at the end for effect. For the idea see *Epistles* I.6.36–7, Lucilius 1194–5W, Juvenal III.143–4. Roman society was indeed one where money could buy prestige and power, and the poet moves swiftly on to a different tack.

63–4 quid facias illi? here means 'what are you to do with a man like that?' **iubeas** is a jussive subjunctive – 'you are to tell him to be miserable since he is so of his own accord'. There is a nice paradox that the miser is happy to be unhappy.

64–7 The misanthropic miser in question was identified by early commentators as Timon of Athens, the contemporary of Pericles and subject of a Shakespeare play (Plutarch *Antony* 70, Cicero *Tusculan Disputations* IV.25, IV.27). The poet here distances himself from the facts with his phrase **ut quidam memoratur** ('as it is said of a certain …'). The dirtiness of the man (**sordidus**) was part of his cynical disdain for (**contemnere**) the manners of society.

66–7 sibilat denotes aggressive 'hissing' as was the custom in the theatre at an unpopular figure on the stage (Cicero *pro Sestio* 115), while **plaudo** continues the theatrical image with the miser applauding himself as he gazes at his own little show of gold. The focus of his attention is his **arca** (money-chest), for which see Juvenal X.25.

68 Tantalus was one of the legendary sinners of ancient mythology: a man of immense wealth who enjoyed the company of the gods at dinner and (in one version of the tale) tested their divine powers by serving up the dismembered body of his own son Pelops as part of the feast: in other accounts he stole the ambrosia and nectar from their dinner table and gave them to mortals. In Homer (*Odyssey* XI.582–92) and in this passage he is doomed to stand in a pool of water which receded when he bent to drink from it, with fruit trees above him which always swung away from him when he reached for them, whereas in Lucretius (III.980–1) he is forced to stand underneath an overhanging rock which constantly threatens to fall on him. The Homeric version of his torment suits Horace better as it illustrates the futility of unfulfilled desire, brought out by phrasing such as **fugientia captat** – 'grasps at what runs away' – as at II.108, Catullus VIII.10.

69 quid rides? ('why are you laughing?' or 'what are you laughing at?') puts laughter into the mouth of the imaginary miser who is amused perhaps by the poet's overdone imagery of Tantalus. Horace is happy to use laughter as part of his strategy for explaining his points (*ridentem dicere verum* I.1.24) and is also happy to expose the laughter of his opponents as really laughter directed at themselves as here ('the tale is told about *you*').

70–2 The miser treats the money bags (**saccis**) as sacred (**sacris**) and goes to sleep over them (**indormis**) with his mouth wide open like Tantalus' (**inhians**) to protect them from use (**parcere**). **cogeris** is promoted to the start of the line for emphasis as it contradicts the statement at 63–4; the miser really is not choosing this behaviour but is compelled by his own greed: money is not his servant but his master. The final image ('to take pleasure in them as if they were painted pictures') is devastating criticism; the money is now reduced to a two-dimensional object with aesthetic value but no inherent use (*usus* – which leads on to the poet's next point).

73 The series of lines beginning with a second-person verb (**indormis ... cogeris**) continues with **nescis. valeat ... praebeat** are both subjunctives in indirect question after **nescis. quo valeat nummus** means 'what cash is good for'. The two phrases are not saying the same thing: *valere* has the sense of being worth in itself, whereas *usum praebere* is to be useful for some practical purpose.

74 The poet rattles off a list of uses for money with asyndeton to enhance the effect of haste and brevity to match the small scale of the desired items. **ematur** is a potential subjunctive – 'might be bought'. The shopping-list is simple fare (as in Horace's meal described in *Satires* I.6.111–18) with a dash of wine thrown in as an extra – a **sextarius** was a liquid measure of about a pint (about half a litre).

75 quis is the shortened form of *quibus* and agrees with **negatis** in an ablative absolute construction. The direct object of the imperative **adde** (74) is omitted but picked up by the relative pronoun, so the phrase runs 'throw in (those things) which, when denied, would make human nature suffer'. The phrasing recalls that of Lucretius II.20–1 and restricts pleasures to those which are natural and necessary; it could be argued that wine (rather than water) is not a necessity but *Odes* III.21 shows deep attachment of this poet to the drink.

76–8 Spending money on food and drink has been recommended in 74–5; the alternative (of storing money safely away from thieves) is now depicted in garishly unattractive terms: one has to lose sleep (**vigilare**), faint with fear (**metu exanimem**) and spend all one's nights and days (**noctesque diesque**) in terror of thieves, fires and slaves. Note the breathless asyndeton of **fures, incendia, servos** as the poet rattles off the fear-list. **noctesque diesque** is hardly needed after **vigilare** but the epic phrasing (and polysyndeton) enhance the intensity of the fear: **malos** might also seem redundant (are there any 'good' thieves?) but here adds a touch of menace to the loss of property. Mention of **servos** is again surprising until we see that the poet is referring to runaways who will take as much as they can carry of your belongings on their way out, and will end up 'fleecing' you (**compilent** is from *pilare* (to 'pluck hairs')). The infinitives (**vigilare … formidare**) are both dependent on **iuvat** ('does this please you, to …?').

78–9 optarim is a subjunctive of cautious assertion: 'I could wish.' **horum … bonorum** is heavily sarcastic of course ('"goods" like these') and is joined to the paradox of the poet 'wishing' to be extremely poor.

80–5 The miser argues that money can buy you care in case of illness – only for the poet to rejoin that his family want the skinflint dead (to inherit his cash). Had the miser been childless, he could have seen himself looked after by a *captator* (legacy-hunter) who would do anything to make the elderly sick man comfortable in order to be left something in the will (see *Satires* II.5, Juvenal XII.93–130). In fact the miser's family will only inherit the vast sums he has built up when he dies and so have no reason to care for him as he has not earned their love (87).

80–1 The man is 'afflicted' (**temptatum**), his body 'has suffered pain' (**condoluit**) with a chill (**frigore**); or some other misfortune (**casus**) has tied him (**adfixit**) to his bed.

81–3 The miser continues the dialogue ('you have') with the poet and gives us a list of the services which his money will buy, all put into final subjunctives ('someone to sit by you …'), with the 'someone' who is the accusative object of **habes** and antecedent for **qui** is omitted. The process begins with simple sitting by the bed (**adsideat**) followed by homely remedies (**fomenta**) and finally the expense of hiring a doctor to put him back on his feet (**suscitet**). The miser assumes that money will 'give back' (**reddat**) the sick man of line 80 to his idealized extended happy family of sons and dear relatives.

84–5 The poet at once pours cold water on this rosy picture with the harsh remarks that even his own wife (**uxor**) does not want the miser healthy (**salvum**), and neither does his son, phrasing this with several short words which accentuate the derision. The poet then widens the scope of the hatred to include 'everybody' (**omnes**) who lives nearby (**vicini**) whom he knows (**noti**): the young generation of both sexes (**pueri atque puellae**) – all these people now positively hate (**oderunt**) him, echoing the miser's own admission at line 66.

86–7 'Are you surprised – when you put money before all else – if nobody offers you a love you don't deserve?' **post … ponas** is a compound verb (*post-ponere*) cut in two by tmesis to emphasize **omnia**, while **praestet** is subjunctive as part of the indirect question after **miraris**. There is rich irony in the monetary metaphor of **merearis**, whose primary meaning is 'to earn money', being applied to this man whose gaining money has 'cost' him the love of his family – a point which the following sentence makes clear.

88–90 This is a difficult passage but much depends on the verbs **velis** and **operam perdas**. One plausible reading understands the poet as saying: 'Do you think that wanting to keep the love of relatives – who came to you from Nature free of charge – is a waste of time and as pointless as saddling a donkey?' The miser thinks that what is freely available must be worthless and any effort expended on it would be

wasted as there is plenty more where that came from. Others see the
poet continuing the theme of the previous sentence and arguing that
for a man as miserable as the miser any effort now to inspire love in
his family would be wasted; and anyway, heaping up money in a bid
to keep the love of family and friends is the wrong way to achieve
this. *operam perdere* means 'to waste one's effort' and when combined
with **infelix** ('a failure') builds up a caricature of the pathetic creature
imagined by the speaker.

89 amicos here is predicative 'keep them as friends' (as well as
relatives).

90–1 The image is of a donkey being saddled up in the Campus Martius
(where Roman cavalry were trained) and expected to gallop with
the horses. The issue is partly one of biology but also of the animal's
refusal to obey the reins (**parentem … frenis**), and the impossibility
of the task is emphasized by the unreal present subjunctive **doceat**
with the indefinite **si quis** ('if someone were to teach').

92 denique marks the poet returning to the main topic after what has
been an entertaining digression ('to summarize') and is reminiscent
of didactic poetry (e.g. Lucretius VI.840). The poet now brings the
text back to more generalized remarks and fewer personal attacks on
a type of individual.

92–3 sit finis quaerendi means 'enough is enough' (literally, 'let
there be a limit to seeking (wealth)') and the poet shows that the fear
of poverty ought to diminish with the increase of wealth, with the
parallel terms **plus … minus** bringing out the correlation. The key
word is **cum-** here which means that 'since' you (by now) have more
money than you need, you can fear poverty less than you did. The
miser could no doubt rejoin that enough is never enough for him as
he has to ensure that he is the richest man in town (cf. 40, 62); the poet

is speaking the language of natural limits, with **finire** in 93 echoing **finis** in 92 and both echoing the need to live within the **fines** of nature (50). **laborem** is a pejorative term for the 'struggle' of seeking wealth and makes the prospect of 'finishing' it all the more pleasant.

94 parto is an ablative absolute understanding *eo* or some such ('now that you have produced (the money)'); it comes from *pario* (which literally means 'to give birth'). The imperfect tense **avebas** is optimistic, assuming that the miser no longer desires what he used to long for. **ne facias quod** (a negative purpose clause) might best be understood as 'to avoid acting like Ummidius …', meaning literally 'so that you won't do [that thing: omitted] which a certain Ummidius [did: omitted]'.

95 Ummidius is not known as a real person – and **quidam** confirms that Horace's readers were not expected to know him. His name is almost certainly significant, perhaps indicating a play on the word *nummi* ('cash') or else a man 'with no moderation' who is going to be chopped up down the middle (**medium**) in line 100. The use of 'significant names' in comedy and satire has a long ancestry from the characters in Aristophanes (e.g. Lysistrata) to the grotesques in Dickens (e.g. Wackford Squeers).

95–9 Horace tells the story briefly in a 'telegram' style, as he promised (**non longa … fabula**). The salient paradoxical points are therefore highlighted and the style is grand in places: he was rich enough to have to weigh his cash as there is too much of it to count, but scruffy enough to pass for a slave, as he was too miserly to spend his cash on clothing: both clauses are consecutive ('so much so that he …'). The phrasing is exactly that used of the Athenian at line 65.

97–8 adusque means the same as *usque ad* (right up to) and the enjambement is nicely expressive of his fear continuing right to the end of his life, here euphemized with **supremum tempus**. **victūs** is genitive singular going with **penuria** ('shortage of livelihood').

99 The two verbs (**opprimeret metuebat**) are juxtaposed to reinforce the idea of the perceived threat and the fear it caused.

99–100 The miser did not in fact die of poverty but was cut in two with an axe wielded by one of his freedwomen; the implication is that he would not have been killed if he had made an effort to be kind to his staff and so was murdered for his miserly ways. Roman slaves could acquire their freedom and become a 'freedman' or 'freedwoman' (**liberta**) and usually (like Cicero's freed slave Tiro) continued to work for their former master. The 'punchline' of the story is that this (presumably Greek) freedwoman, elevated to the status of Clytemnestra (the 'strongest of the daughters of Tyndareus'), murdered her master – as Clytemnestra murdered her husband Agamemnon – with an axe. The epic scale of the miser's death is well conveyed in the four-word line, ending with the resonant superlative (**fortissima**) and the patronymic term **Tyndaridarum.** There is significance in the man being cut down the middle as he was one who lived in extremes (of miserly squalor and of massive wealth) and so was cut down with the 'middle way' or 'golden mean' which he had spent his life spurning and which the poet will advocate in the following lines. **divisit** is also apt for one who was **dives** (95), as is the irony that his death was brought about by someone who (unlike Ummidius) was free (**liberta**).

101–21: Wasting money foolishly as a spendthrift is just as bad as being a miser and the poet recommends moderation in all things and recapitulates his earlier argument that discontentment with their status (both personal and financial) makes people unhappy and unable to see the good things they could enjoy.

I.3

The first poem in the collection concerned itself with our avarice and discontent and in particular how the miser can never be truly happy or loved. The second poem concerned our attitude towards sex and again the theme is one of avoiding extremes and pursuing sensible moderation in all things, avoiding both fastidiousness at one end of the spectrum and total lack of taste at the other. This third in the series of 'diatribe' satires concerns friendship – keeping one's friends and seeing good friends as a part of the happy life.

Satire is often seen as harsh criticism of others by sneering mockery, such as Lucilius who 'scoured the city with his abundant wit' (Horace *Satires* I.10.3–4), but the argument in this poem is rather one of tolerance and indulgence: be kind to yourself and others, as 'nobody is born without faults' (68). We should apply the same kinder interpretation of the faults of others as we do to those of ourselves, and not be quick to exonerate our own behaviour while excoriating others. There is mockery in the poem, but it is a gentle exposé of the ways in which lovers and parents indulge the obvious flaws of the people they love (38–48), and light self-mockery of the poet's own clumsy interrupting of the great man Maecenas when he is busy (64–5). In the second half of the poem Horace aims his critical mirth at the Stoic ideas of justice and wisdom, putting his own concept of the carefree indulgent life of friendship as superior to that of the Stoic 'king' in his threadbare loneliness.

Summary of the poem

This poem begins (1–19) with a comic sketch of the singer Tigellius as a man of infuriating extremes – he would sing when not needed and refuse to sing when required, he would sleep in the day and be awake at night, and so on: Horace then (20–37) attacks the tendency to be too indulgent with ourselves while criticizing other people. We ought to be indulgent towards the faults of others as lovers and parents are (38–48) and put a kind construction on others' behaviour and characters (49–67) as we are all flawed and need to be aware of our own flaws as well as those of others (68–75). We should not over-react to small offences (76–95) and the authoritarian Stoic idea that all crimes are equal is held up to scorn and ridicule (96–124). The poet then (124–33) mocks the Stoic idea that the wise man is 'king' who can do anything with a wonderful *reductio ad absurdum* (133–42) of the Stoic sage as a self-styled 'king' being mocked on his way to the baths while our carefree poet goes along with his friends, living 'more happily than Your Majesty'.

1–24: This poem begins with a comic sketch of the singer Tigellius as a man of infuriating extremes, and then attacks the tendency to be too indulgent with ourselves while criticizing other people.

25–8 We need to be indulgent towards our friends' faults and less complacent about ourselves. The contrast is drawn between our sharp-eyed view of others and the bleary myopic attention we pay to our own faults – a contrast familiar to us from Jesus' comparison of our seeing the motes in the eyes of others but missing the beams in our own eyes (Matthew 7.3).

25 *lippitudo* and *aspritudo* (trachoma) were relatively common ailments in ancient Rome and feature regularly in literature (cf. I.120, VII.3: Horace says he is a sufferer at V.30); the condition is something akin to conjunctivitis. The term is used metaphorically here of a lack of clarity of vision and the visual impairment is emphasized by the juxtaposition **lippus inunctis** where the disease and the treatment (smearing with ointment) will both combine to stop us seeing clearly. **mala** here means 'bad qualities'.

26 in here means 'in the case of' and **acutum** is adverbial neuter ('sharply'). Eagles were (and are) proverbially sharp-eyed and the Greeks also regarded the snake (*drakon*) as sharp-sighted, its name derived from *derkesthai* (to see). **serpens Epidaurius** refers to the medical site Epidaurus where the god of healing (Asclepius) was worshipped in the form of a snake; the adjective makes the simple animal analogy more specific and emphatic.

27–8 contra is adverbial ('on the other hand') and **ēvĕnit** is a vivid present tense, juxtaposed with **inquirant** to bring out the immediacy of the reciprocal examination of faults. **inquirant** is subjunctive in a result clause ('it turns out for you that …'). **illi** refers to the friends of line 26. Note how the poet's view of his faults termed them **mala** ('bad qualities') while your friends correctly term them **vitia** ('vices').

29–34 The poet gives a quick character sketch of an unidentified character: but hints elsewhere in his poetry strongly support the idea that he is describing himself.

29 iracundior is a comparative qualified by **paulo**, with the sense 'a little bit more irascible (than the average)' and so 'somewhat irascible', as he admits in *Epistles* I.20.25.

29–30 'Less suited to the sharp noses of these men' means 'less able to fit into the snobbish climate of today'. The nose was associated with critical judgement in general (e.g. I.4.8) and in particular scorn or anger (*Epistles* I.5.23, I.19.45). Here the judgement is metaphorically 'sharp' (**acutis**), as at line 26, and the poet gives a typically vivid image of sniffy society 'looking down its nose' at him; the reasons for his perceived lack of acceptance are suggested in the lines that follow.

30–2 The man does not look right. 'He could be mocked because he has a bumpkin's haircut, his toga hangs down and his loose sandal is flapping off his foot.' **rusticius** is the comparative adverb of *rusticus* (cf. **parcius** line 49) and is going with **tonso** which is the dative of the perfect participle passive ('in the case of the man with a haircut', **tonso** being a dative of possession); and so means 'with his hair cut in a more rustic manner'. The subject of the main verb **defluit** is **toga** (as **calceus** is subject of **haeret**); the syntax perfectly recreates the superficial critique which gives pride of place to the toga and the sandal rather than the man wearing them. Horace tells us in his *Epistles* (I.1.94–6) that his haircut is uneven and his toga hangs down askew, and the 'slipshod' sandal is also a feature of the clown and the oafish peasant: it all reminds us of the other-worldly untidiness of a Socrates or of the Cynic philosophers such as Diogenes. **eo** is the same as *ideo* ('for that reason').

32–4 If the outward appearance is awful, the inner man is good, almost in inverse proportion. **bonus, ut melior** [*sit*] is a consecutive clause ('he is good, to the extent that there is nobody else better …'). **ingenium ingens** ('massive talent') is a neat play on words suggesting a link between the two and also allowing both to hint at a contrast between what is 'in-born' (*in-gen-*) and what is superficial (**inculto … corpore**). **tibi** could be taken as referring to Maecenas himself (who was nothing if not fastidious in his dress and social habits) or else to the reader, and the moral 'don't judge by appearances' is coupled with the satirist's adopting a *persona* of the 'misfit' outsider in society.

34–6 denique cf. I.92n. **te ipsum / concute** is a peremptory imperative to the reader drawing his attention back to himself and away from the man who is the focus of 29–34. **concute** means 'shake your clothing' to find what is hidden in the folds; there is an implied verb before **num** ('(to find out) whether …'). **quă** is the alternative form of *quae* used indefinitely (**num qua vitiorum** = *num quae vitia* 'whether any vices'). The agricultural metaphors are strong here: **inseverit** from *insero* ('I sow') and **natura** ('nature') both leading the poet to suggest a pun of **vitiorum** (vices) and *viciarum* ('vetch'). **olim** broadens the scope of the inquiry ('at any time') and then **consuetudo mala** ('bad habits') allows for the vices to be developed rather than inborn.

37 The agricultural image is roundly concluded with a piece of generalized wisdom (a so-called 'gnomic' utterance) declaring a farmer's truism: neglect your fields and you will have to burn out the ferns that grow in them. The rural lore is apt coming from a man with a rustic haircut (31).

38–40 Horace now turns from the harsh criticism of faults to their indulgence by lovers. **illuc praevertamur ... quod** is a iussive subjunctive ('let us turn our attention to the fact that ...'). The lover and his girlfriend are placed close to each other in line 38 and the pejorative terms are all grouped together in line 39 (**turpia decipiunt caecum vitia**). Love is famously blind (Catullus 67.25, Lucretius IV.1120) but here the poet makes the lover perverse in his 'delight' (**delectant**) in the girl's flaws. The mockery of lovers' blindness to the obvious flaws in their beloved had been memorably done by Plato (*Republic* 474d–e) and Lucretius (IV.1153–70), and Horace develops the theme with imagery of indulgent parents (43–8) and kind friends (49–54) rather than simply to revisit the Lucretian imagery of foppish boyfriends. What is folly to the philosophers is recommended here by the satirist.

40 pōlypus (*poulupous* in Greek) is a nasal tumour or polyp. The names of the couple are well chosen: **Balbinum** suggests *balbus* ('lisping', used of old men at *Epistles* I.20.18) and *balbutire* ('to stammer', cf. 48) suggestive of a nervous pathetic lover, while **Hagnae** is clearly derived from Greek *hagnos* ('pure', 'holy') suggestive of the lover's idealized image of her as contrasted with her facial faults.

41-2 vellem … erraremus is colloquial in tone ('I would like us to make the same sort of mistake …'). The poet quickly repeats the key concept in **erraremus … errori** and the tone puts an ironic spin on the word: 'I wish … that virtue had applied an honourable name to that "mistake".'

43-4 Fathers are often less critical of their own children and Horace sees this as a model for the behaviour of friends. The construction is clear: 'as a father (does not show revulsion towards) any fault there may be in a son of his, so we ought not to feel revulsion towards any fault in a friend.' **amici** and **gnati** are both genitive singular.

44-53 A lively sequence of euphemisms used by fathers alongside the more pejorative descriptions. The passage is modelled in style on Lucretius' satire of lovers' euphemisms at IV.1160-70: both poets mention a short euphemistic term of affection (e.g. here **pullum, varum, scaurum**) only to unpack it in brutal anatomical terms. Horace then goes on to discuss the relativity of character judgements – in modern terms, one man's terrorist is another man's freedom-fighter; my convictions are your prejudices; I am a man of firm opinions, you are just stubborn. This is reminiscent of the passage in Thucydides (III.82) where the impact of civil war in Corcyra was to change the meanings of value-terms in this way.

44-5 strabo ('squinting') and **paetus** ('having a cast in the eye') both indicate being cross-eyed, but **strabo** was less desirable and more extreme than **paetus** which seems to have been a mark of the goddess Venus.

45-6 A *pullus* is a chicken and can mean 'little darling': **male** gives the extra edge of nastiness to the smallness ('badly stunted') and the poet then indulges in more gratuitous mockery of the child with the word

abortivus ('prematurely born' and so 'a runt') and ending the phrase with the name **Sisyphus** (47) in enjambement, referring to a famous dwarf of Mark Antony.

47–8 Horace again loads the description; **varum** indicates 'knock-kneed' and does not sound so bad, whereas the crude reality is that his 'legs are twisted': **scaurum** again is 'swollen-ankled' and the word is neutral, while the harsh nature of the deformity is that he finds it hard (**male**) to be supported (**fultum**) on his 'bent ankles'. The verb **balbutit** indicates the father's affectionate 'lisping' or 'cooing' over his child.

49–53 After three examples of indulgent parents, Horace gives us four examples of indulgent friends making excuses for the poor behaviour of their *amici*; in each case the harsh reality is stated first followed by the kinder account of the same behaviour.

49 frugi (formed as the predicative dative from *frux*) functions as an indeclinable adjective meaning 'sensible, honest' and is the nicer way to describe the man who lives 'more parsimoniously' (**parcius** is the comparative adverb from *parcus*). **ineptus** denotes 'silly' or inappropriate behaviour (cf. Catullus VIII.1) and derives from *in-aptus*.

50–1 *iactare se* is to 'show off' and is already a negative form of self-assertion, made even worse by the comparative form **iactantior**: it leads neatly to the verb **postulat** ('he claims' or even 'demands') which shows him trying to force others to share his self-image of being **concinnus** or 'good company'.

51–3 The theme of outspokenness continues: the reality is of an over-aggressive (**truculentior**) man who speaks his mind more freely than he needs, but who is to be regarded as 'frank and fearless'. **habeatur**

and **numeretur** are jussive subjunctives ('let him be regarded as ... let him be counted amongst ...').

53 caldior is the shorter form of *calidior* and denotes 'hot-headed': Horace postpones the preposition **inter** (as at I.1.47) after **acres** which here means 'forceful' or 'dynamic'.

54 Horace again rounds off the section with a gnomic line (cf. 37) making a generalization. The polyptoton **iungit iunctos** is effective in enhancing the image of the union of the friends, as is the balanced parallel phrasing of: verb + accusative et verb + accusative. The second **et** is postponed, so that the line is to be understood as follows: **haec res et iungit et iunctos servat amicos**, that is, 'this sort of thing joins people together and preserves their union once they are friends', with **iunctos** agreeing with **amicos** and being the object of **servat**.

55–67 Horace has praised the practice of making allowances for friends with kind interpretations of their faults: now he exposes how we actually do the opposite and cynically treat even good qualities of others as being vices of one sort or another. The 'topsy-turvy' world is brought out by the verb **invertimus** ('we turn virtues on their heads').

56 The image is of a wine-jar (**vas**) which is clean (**sincerum**) but which we positively want (**cupimus**) to stain (**incrustare**). The verb *incrustare* can mean to 'plaster over' (and so repair cracks) which would make sense as we are mad to 'repair' a jar which is not cracked: but this does not fit the context of people creating flaws where none exist, and ancient critics saw it as rather the poet allowing foul sour wine to line the inside of a clean jar. This better fits the idea of tarnishing the clean.

56–8 The good qualities are described at greater length than the hurtful judgements: this neatly shows the rapid dismissing of a good man in a few harsh words, and the poet includes himself in this bad behaviour with the first person plural verbs **damus** (58), **vocamus** (62), **inquimus** (66) and **sancimus** (67).

56-7 quis here means the same as *aliquis* ('someone'). **nobiscum vivit** is not to be taken too literally and may simply means 'lives in our circle of society'. **demissus** indicates modest humility, cynically interpreted as lack of energy.

57-8 The final syllable of **homo** is elided into **illi** despite the punctuation between the two words. The pejorative terms **tardo** ('slow') and **pingui** ('thick') are piled up with asyndeton and show the instant condemnation of the man with a name which will stick. *cognomina* were additional names whose origins were often personal characteristics, such as Paetus ('squinting'), Naso ('big nose'): see OCD s.v. 'names, personal, Roman'. **tardo** and **pingui** are here attracted into the dative case agreeing with **illi**.

58-62 The second example shows how prudent self-protection is seen as insincerity and cunning.

58-9 The poet loads the description by depicting the scene as almost a war zone where self-protection is obviously sensible. *insidiae* ('traps') are by definition to be avoided, as is anybody who is **malo** – and the language of **latus obdit apertum** (literally 'offers an exposed flank') is military.

60-1 The language of the previous two lines has already established the sound sense of this behaviour, but the poet goes on here to depict the milieu itself (**genus hoc ... vitae**) as being hostile and productive of self-defence mechanisms. Note the transposition of **inter** (as at I.1.47, I.3.53) and the telling enjambement of **acris / invidia** throwing stress on the noun, as well as the anaphora of **ubi** with hyperbaton in the second

phrase. This is rhetorical pleading of an (ironic?) intensity and some
commentators have assumed that the poet here refers to his own calling
of a writer of satire, although there is no explicit evidence for this in the
text and Horace is careful to keep his point general rather than personal.

61–2 pro here means 'instead of' and one imagines the 'correct'
interpretations as being in quotes: 'instead of (calling him) "sensible"
and "cautious" we call him …' The poet again loads the terms nicely:
bene sano is vague but undeniably positive, while the litotes **non
incauto** (= *cauto*) is itself an understatement suggesting that he is
only lacking in what would be another cause for reproach.

62 As at 56–8, the truth of the previous four lines is dismissed in
two harsh cynical adjectives. **fictum** (from the perfect participle
passive from *fingo*) denotes sham insincerity – Virgil uses it of
the traitor Sinon in *Aeneid* II.107 – while **astutum** is also used in
Horace's *Satires* of the crafty legacy-hunter at II.5.23 and the sly fox
at II.3.186.

63–7 Here the poet does present something of his own experience, as
is clear from 63–4. The ebullient chatterer who speaks when others
are enjoying a quiet moment is seen as lacking in consideration and
is the opposite of the wary individual of 59 who offers his 'exposed
flank to no man'. Here the poet allows for more(self-) criticism in the
terms he uses and he also scales down the cynical judgement to avoid
offending his patron.

63 The key word **simplicior** is promoted for emphasis to the start
of the line and the sentence: for the comparative form see **parcius**
(49), **iactantior** (50), **truculentior** (51). *simplex* indicates (as at 52) an
uncomplicated and straightforward manner and (here, when joined
to **molestus** (65)) *gaucherie* – elsewhere it denotes artlessness (*Odes*
I.5.5). **quis** here means *aliquis* and it is tempting to hear the burbling

intruder's language mocked in the tumbling sequence of **quis et est qualem**, where we have to understand *talis* before **qualem**.

63–5 The autobiographical element becomes explicit (**me … tibi, Maecenas**) and also cleverly implicit (**sermone**: *sermones* is the title given to this book of poems).

64 obtulerim is a perfect subjunctive indicating a wish, a meaning brought out by the combination with **saepe libenter** (63): 'the sort of character I would be glad to think I have shown you on many occasions.' For **Maecenas** see the Introduction. **ut** introduces a result clause depending on an understood *talis* (the sort of man to …).

64–5 legentem aut tacitum ('reading or being silent') has been taken to suggest that Romans read aloud to themselves, but may mean simply 'reading or enjoying a quiet moment'. The point is not the contrast between the two activities but the sharp contrast between both and the sudden unwelcome interruption with 'some *sermo* or other', using the self-deprecating **quovis**. The violence of the interruption is brought out by **impellat … molestus. legentem aut tacitum** agrees with the unspecified person who is the object of **impellat**. Maecenas was not the only victim of the poet's *gauche* behaviour.

66 communi sensu is not 'common sense' but rather 'feeling for the general good of others' or just 'fellow-feeling'. The poet is quick to include himself in this (self-) criticism with the plural verb **inquimus**, only to realize what he is doing and lament the whole business (**eheu**). For this sort of modest self-analysis see II.3.323, *Epistles* I.20.20–25, Catullus X.

67 'how rash we are to enact a law which is unfair against ourselves!' The suffix **-met** adds a touch of emphatic grandeur to the phrase **legem sancimus**.

68–9 The order for translation is: *nemo nascitur sine vitiis.* The generalization has the effect of throwing the critique back in the face of the critic – nobody is born without faults, not even you. The **optimus** man is the one who is 'beset' by **minimis** faults – and **minimis** means both 'smallest' and also 'least in number'.

69–72 A 'sweet friend' ought to weigh up the good features against the bad and allow the former to compensate for the latter. The value-terms are loaded – not just an **amicus** but one who is **dulcis**, that is, one with genuine affection rather than simply a political ally, and **aequum** picks up the imagery of **iniquam** in 67.

70 cum is the preposition ('with', to be taken with **vitiis**) and not the conjunction. The present subjunctives **compenset** and **inclinet** (71) are both jussive ('let him …'). The key terms **vitiis** and **bona** are juxtaposed for contrasting effect. The image in **hisce … inclinet** is of 'tipping the scales' in favour of 'these' more numerous virtues (i.e. the **bona**), and is somewhat ironic in view of **aequum** (69) which means both 'fair' and also (in the case of scales) 'balanced' and so the best scales for weighing friends are those which are actually crooked in favour of the good. The 'scales' imagery concludes with **trutina** ('balance') in 72. The -**ce** suffix on **hisce** is the so-called 'deictic particle' which adds emphasis to *his.*

71–2 amari si volet gives the friend a motive for behaving thus, and once again suggests that it is self-interested to be indulgent towards others as the friend will be 'put into the same balance'. **ponetur** is an assertive future indicative.

73–4 Translate thus: 'the man, who expects (**postulat**) his friend not to be upset by his own tumours, will pardon (the friend's) warts.' **propriis** denotes 'belonging to oneself' and refers to the subject of the main verb, while **illius** refers to 'that (friend)'. The reciprocal understanding is again loaded in that the faults of the friend are as nothing compared with those of the other man, and takes us back to the sentiments of 25–8.

74–5 The point concludes with a neat summary of the need for mutual understanding between friends with the paired alliteration (**peccatis ... poscentem reddere rursus**) suggesting the reciprocity, and the key word **rursus** (derived from *reversus*) placed with **reddere** and emphasized at the end of the line and the sentence.

76–133: The poem ends with an attack on the Stoics for their idea that all offences are equal and also for their statement that the wise man is king. The poet is happy with his less judgemental friends than the Stoic 'wise man'.

II.2

The second book of *Satires* opened with a poem discussing the function of satire – a poem which acts as a preface to the second book and may well have been composed later than the other seven poems in the book. The second poem in the book concerns itself with the familiar satirical topic of the simple life (**victus tenuis** 70), with especial reference to food, and with something of a political edge in that it concerns a farmer who has lost his land to one of Octavian's veterans. Food is something of an obsession in this second book of *Satires*, being discussed in poems 2, 4, 6 and 8.

Summary of the poem

The poem begins with a discussion of what makes food good. Not the outer appearance or the exotic provenance (you do not eat the flashy feathers (27–8)), but the hunger which requires feeding – 'seek your sauce by sweat'. The hungry man does not turn his nose up at plain food and snobbery about food is misguided. The poet then turns to the opposite extreme from conspicuous affluence, that is conspicuous meanness, such as only eating food which is rotten or drinking wine which has gone off. Wisdom is found in the moderation and good sense to eat sensibly; and the poem then lists some of the health benefits of eating in moderation. The poem ends with an inspiring passage on the mutability of life and the way in which we are all in some ways borrowers of what we regard as ours: even the bodies we live in are made of atoms which we will have to give back to the world from which we came.

1–4 The poem opens as a lecture on moral philosophy, complete with a Platonic manner of address to the audience as 'good men' (cf. Plato *Laws* 684e, *Protagoras* 314d). The style is didactic, with the main verb **discite** postponed until line 4 and the object of the learning contained in the indirect question in line 1, as in the opening lines of Virgil's *Georgics* and of Manilius' *Astronomica*.

1 The subject is not **virtus** in general but 'what sort of **virtus** – and how great a sort of **virtus** – it is to live on a little'. For the Epicurean motto of living on the 'little that is enough' (*parvum quod satis est*) see Lucretius V.1118–19; Epicurus himself was said to be content with bread and water, asking to be sent a pot of cheese so that he could 'dine sumptuously' now and then (Diogenes Laertius X.11); and austerity was also practised by philosophers such as Socrates and lauded elsewhere by poets idealizing rural simplicity (e.g. *Epistles* II.1.139 (*fortes parvoque beati*), Virgil *Georgics* II.467–74, Tibullus I.1.25, Juvenal XI.77–89). **parvo** is ablative of means (AG §409): 'on a little'.

2 These poems are entitled *sermones* ('conversations' or 'chats') and so there is a nice irony in the poet saying that this *sermo* (poem) is not his own *sermo* (conversation). The poet distances himself from the advice being offered, as he also does in the dialogue form of II.3 and II.7 and as Juvenal does in his *Satire* 3. **Ofellus** sounds like a significant name as *ofella* is a small meatball (Juvenal XI.144) as eaten by a poor man.

3 The whole line is given over to a three-part description of **Ofellus** (2). *norma* means a 'standard' or 'pattern' and so **abnormis** (*ab-normis*) means 'irregular' or 'not belonging to any school of philosophy'. The term **rusticus** also denoted the unschooled and unsophisticated (cf. I.3.31) and so the two words juxtaposed lead nicely to the surprising term **sapiens** ('wise') after the caesura. **crassa … Minerva** is a play on words. Minerva was the goddess of wisdom and so her name could stand for 'wisdom' itself (a device known as 'metonymy') in which case the phrase means 'with coarse wisdom': but Minerva was also the goddess of weaving and so the phrase can also suggest the coarse weave of his rustic clothing.

4–7 The lesson is to be learned not at a banquet but before lunch (**impransi**) when the mind is more alert. The learning process is marked by the two imperatives which frame this passage (**discite … disquirite**).

4–6 The Roman banquet is satirized as all glitter and glamour, with shining dishes and tables, the diner's vision (**acies**) blinded with the shining (**fulgoribus**) and the heart (**animus**) rejecting the better course of action (**meliora** – 'better things'). **acclinis** is here nominative agreeing with **animus** and taken with **falsis** ('when the mind is inclining towards fake appearances'). The dinner party stupefies our senses and moves our hearts when we need to apply our minds; and the poet will go on to show how we are deceived by a glamorous exterior masking a plain substance underneath when he describes luxury foods (19–28).

7 After the lengthy three-line description of the dinner, the poet's actual situation is as simple as its description ('here before lunch' **hic impransi**). **disquirite** occurs only here in Latin and the rare verb suggests an academic or judicial investigation. The speaker of the question **'cur hoc?'** is presumably one of the **boni** addressed in line 1, to whom Horace replies **'dicam si potero'** in the next line.

8–9 'Any judge who has been bribed is bad at weighing up what is true.' The sentence is metaphorical here for the way in which our minds can be 'bribed' by pleasure into assenting to what is wrong.

9–15 The sentence is a long series of phrases strung together in a loose syntactical structure. The essential meaning comes out at the end: 'when you are tired out with hard physical effort, then try rejecting plain food.' Lines 9–13 assembles a list of possible ways of becoming tired, the catalogue of exhausting pursuits delivered in suitably breathless haste in which the poet fails to supply all the words needed to fill out the sentence and in which the variation of activities and construction maintains our attention and interest.

9–10 equo / ... ab indomito means 'from [riding] a horse which has not been broken in'.

10–11 The contrast here is between Roman military exercise (**militia**) and the Greek softness which would find it hard going. **graecari** ('to behave like a Greek') is somewhat pejorative: mockery of the Greeks – and especially mockery of the use of Greek words in Latin – seems to have been something of a standard feature of satire (cf. Juvenal *Satires* III.58–125, Persius VI. 38–40) and of Plautine comedy. The order for translating these lines is: *si Romana militia fatigat [te] adsuetum graecari* ('If Roman military exercise tires [you], accustomed [as you are] to behaving like a Greek'). Horace has started the sentence with a nominative singular subject understood (**sectatus** line 9) but the parenthesis (**vel si ... disco** (10–13)) assumes that that nominative subject is now the accusative **te** who is the object of the verb **fatigat** (whose subject is **militia**) and who then becomes the subject of the second-person imperatives **pete** (13) and **sperne** (15).

11–12 The **pila** was a ball, popular in Greek sport and line 12 well captures the way the pleasure of the sport softly tricks the exerciser into doing more exercise, literally 'with the enthusiasm softly tricking the hard work' in an ablative absolute construction. There is a neat oxymoron of **molliter austerum**, the latter term borrowed from Greek to depict the harshness of the sport.

13 The discus-throw was the athletic event started by the Greeks and immortalized for us in the statue of the *discobolos* of Myron, a copy of which is to be found in the British Museum: see the astonishing throw of Odysseus in Homer *Odyssey* VIII.186–200. The phrase means 'if the discus stirs you into action' and is then followed by apparently direct speech addressed to the discus-thrower. The final two words of the line make up the final two feet, with **aera** scanned $\bar{a}\breve{e}r\breve{a}$ and final syllable of **cedentem** swallowed in elision before **aera**. There is notable assonance of 'e' in **te ... pete cedentem**.

14 The detail of the preceding lines is now summed up in a single line with suitably breathless asyndeton, apt adjectives for thirst ('dry' **siccus**) and hunger ('empty' **inanis**) along with a powerful metaphor 'hammered out your fussiness' (**extuderit** from *extundo*).

15-16 The need for food and drink prompts this challenge: 'try rejecting cheap food [then]' that is when you are **siccus** (14) and **inanis** (14). The thirst can be assuaged with anything and the poet mocks the very idea of refusing to drink any wine that is not Falernian (the name of the vintage indicating the voice of the connoisseur) mixed with honey from Mt Hymettus in Greece, a combination which produced *mulsum* – a form of mead served up with the first course of a Roman dinner. Here it is notable that the exotic honey is diluted with the wine rather than vice versa. **ne** + perfect subjunctive indicates a prohibition and the sense is: 'don't drink [anything at all] unless it is honey.' Notice the poet's strong use of two forms of the imperative in his hectoring, dominant style of address.

16 The **promus** was the slave in the household who 'brings out' (*promit*) food and drink from the stores: if he were out (with the keys) then the food in the stores would be unavailable.

16-17 Fish is unavailable as the 'black sea is stormy, protecting the fish'. **defendens** is a nice pathetic fallacy endowing the sea with the purpose of safeguarding its fish, and **atrum ... hiemat** gives a vivid picture of the black storm clouds darkening the sea.

17-18 Bread and salt will suffice, the two items juxtaposed on the line as they are on the plate. **latrantem** (literally 'barking' like a dog) used of the growling and rumbling of the stomach reminds us of the Cynics (whose name *kynikos* means 'dog-like') and also of Homer *Odyssey* VII.216 ('nothing is more dog-like (i.e. shameless) than the stomach') XX.13-16, Lucretius II.17. The assonance of 'a' in **sale panis / latrantem** perhaps evokes the barking of the dog.

18-19 The reader is imagined asking the poet for more information. **unde** ('from where?') and **qui** ('how?') go with **partum** (from *pario*) so that the phrase means 'from what source or by what means do you think this (effect is) produced?' **unde** asks for the cause, while **qui** asks for the mechanism by which cheap food will satisfy you.

19-20 The poet asserts that the pleasure is not in the 'expensive aroma' (**caro nidore**) of the food but is in oneself. For the savouring of the smell of cooking food see II.1.38, Juvenal V.162: certainly bread and salt will not have the tempting aroma of (say) roast meat. The argument is Epicurean in tone: the **voluptas summa** was the goal of Epicurean ethics which stated that the greatest good was in fact pleasure. The smell of the food does not satisfy us as the atoms which excite the nose will not fill the stomach, and it is only when the food is actually inside us (**in te ipso**) that we feel the real pleasure (see Lucretius IV.627-32 for the mechanics of nutrition and how pleasure fits into this). Compared with this, the expensive aroma is devoid of real pleasure.

20-1 The poet addresses the reader with a jab (**tu**) and tells him to 'seek your sauce by sweat' - one of Horace's most effective aphorisms. **pulmentaria** were 'relish' or anything tasty to be eaten with plain bread. The sentiment that 'hunger is the best sauce' was also attributed to Socrates (Xenohon *Memorabilia* I.3.5) but Horace makes it especially sharp by his use of the peremptory personal pronoun (**tu**, not long after **te**) and by the labouring heavy syllables of **sūdāndō** emphasized in enjambement.

21-2 The glutton who thinks he loves his food does not in fact get the real pleasure as he is not hungry enough to enjoy it all properly (cf. Cicero *Tusculan Disputations* V.99-100). The subjects of the verb **poterit** are the several forms of exotic foodstuffs (**ostrea ... scarus ... peregrina lagois** - all three transliterated Greek words). The verb is in the singular: the three foods are all different forms of the same thing (exotic food) and the singular verb also lends force to the final climactic item (**peregrina ... lagois**) (see AG §317b and cf. *Odes* I.22.20). The gourmand is quickly described in three consecutive words as 'fat and pale with his excesses' and the extent of his gluttony is expansively shown in the increasingly rare foods. **ostrea** is an oyster, much prized as luxury food (cf. Juvenal VIII.85–6, XI.49), while the **scarus** is the 'parrot-wrasse' fish which could only be fished in Italian waters if storms had driven it from its natural habitat in the east and which was noted for its size and taste. The *pièce de résistance*, the **lagois**, was a form of grouse and is probably the *lagopus muta* or 'Rock Ptarmigan': Pliny says this bird could not be kept outside its Alpine habitat which lends real force to 'foreign'. **ostrea** is scanned as two syllables with the *-ea* ending treated as a diphthong, a device known as 'synizesis'.

23 The construction is 'I will not save you (**eripiam**) from wanting (**velis quin**) to ...' **eripiam** acts as verb of prohibition which takes **quin** + subjunctive.

23–4 The contrast is between the peacock (**pavone**) and the chicken (**gallina**). For the argument see I.2.114–16 ('when thirst burns your throat, do you demand golden cups? when hungry do you turn your nose up at everything except peacock and turbot?'). **posito pavone** is an ablative absolute ('once the peacock has been served') driving a wedge between the poet's saving help (**eripiam**) and your desire (**velis**). **tergere palatum** literally means 'to rub the palate' and sounds like the sort of pretentious culinary phrasing which satire likes to mock.

25 vanis rerum here means *vanis rebus* like *vilia rerum* at *Epistles* I.15.21 and *abdita rerum* in *Ars Poetica* 49. The construction of the neuter of the adjective acting as a noun, coupled with a defining partitive genitive is found in elevated Latin poetry: cf. *Odes* IV.12.19–20,

Virgil *Aeneid* I.422, Lucretius IV.415, VI.809. The effect here is to throw the emphasis on to the word **vanis** – it is not the 'things' which have corrupted you but their empty outward show. **corruptus** reminds us of the **iudex** in 9.

25–6 Price equates to value, says the world: the meat sells for gold and so must be worth more than the cheap chicken – and peacocks were especially valuable commodities. The phrase 'rare bird' becomes proverbial – cf. Juvenal VI.165, Persius I.46 – but here is literally meant. The phrasing of 'spreads out public shows with its painted tail' – with the metaphors of **picta** and **spectacula** and the 'p' alliteration – is suitably impressive to make the point.

27 'as though (that) had anything at all to do with the matter'.

27–8 The satirist forces us to confront the reality with a disgusting image of eating feathers. The argument is that foodstuffs are valuable only as food. The peacock's feathers make it prettier but no better as food than chicken and so, unless you eat the feathers, the peacock is no better as food. As the earlier satirist Lucilius (761–2W) put it: 'the cook does not care that the tail is amazing so long as the bird is fat.'

28 num would normally elide before a following vowel (*n(um) adest*) but here there is a hiatus so that it scans **nŭm ădest**. **honor** here indicates 'beauty' or 'distinction' of appearance as at *Odes* II.11.9–10, Lucretius IV.1163, Virgil *Aeneid* I.591: **cocto** (past participle passive from *coqueo*) is in the possessive dative case with **adest** ('the same beauty is to the cooked thing', that is, 'does it keep its beauty once it is cooked?').

29–30 The construction is that of an exclamatory infinitive (as in *Epode* VIII.1) with **te** as its subject: 'yet although there is no difference (**distat nil**) in their meat – to think that you, deceived by the differing appearances, should go for that one rather than this one!' **esto** is a third-person imperative from *sum* ('let it be', that is, 'very well then').

31–69: The poet continues his rebuttal of the quest for luxury in dining (31–52) and then (53–69) turns to the opposite vice to gluttony, that is, meanness and living on scraps, in order to dismiss this also.

70–93 Ancient philosophy aimed to improve our lives in practical ways, and the poet now turns to the health benefits of the moderate diet he has been advocating.

70–1 accipe is addressed to the reader in a didactic manner and is the main verb, with the indirect questions **quae … adferat** the subject-matter which the reader is to 'take in'. Horace repeats the phrase **quae quantaque** from line 1, a repetition which contributes towards unifying the poem and making the coherence of the different sections more obvious.

71–2 valeas is a subjunctive functioning as a potential – 'you could be healthy (if you lived as I tell you)', a construction which continues with **credas** ('(if you do as I say) you would then believe that a variety of foods do damage to a man'). **imprimis** derives from *in primis* and means 'above all'; health matters more than any more philosophical considerations.

72 A mixture of different sorts of cooked food all eaten together was regarded by some ancient writers as harmful to health as the different foods would be digested at different speeds – and there was also a perception that *haute cuisine* masked unhealthy food to make it taste good, such as in Plato's contrast of medicine with cookery in terms of real health vs meretricious 'goodness' in *Gorgias* 465c. As often, this is at variance with the parallel idea that a meal made up of a kaleidoscopic array of foods (such as we see in Trimalchio's feast in Petronius or Virro's banquet in Juvenal 5) was the height of luxury and elegance.

72–3 In contrast to the **variae res** (71) is the preferred singular **escae** which, because it was **simplex**, 'sat well' (*OLD* s.v. 'sedeo' 8) and so did not gurgle or cause **tumultum** (75) in the stomach. **olim** means here 'in the past' and **tibi** is in the dative of advantage, meaning here little more than 'in your case'; the whole passage is addressed to a 'you' who is the reader in the second-person verbs (**accipe ... valeas ... credas ... vides**). **ut** here means 'how'; translate: 'you could believe how harmful a variety of foods are to a man when you recall ...'

73–6 The construction is a simple conditional with future perfect in the protasis after **simul** ('as soon as you mix ...') and then future indicatives in the apodosis (**vertent ... feret**).

assis ('roasted') denotes dry cooking while **elixa** ('boiled') indicates wet cooking. This sort of mixing of two opposite elements does not sound odd for those of us who eat boiled potatoes with roast beef but is part of the general theme of incongruity. The poet then singles out the eating together of shellfish with thrushes (wet and dry creatures) and asserts that the 'sweetness' will turn to 'bile' and 'the sluggish phlegm will bring rioting in the stomach'. Thrushes were eaten in Roman banquets and were cheap to obtain – cf. I.5.72, *Epistles* I.15.40–1 ('nothing better than a fat thrush'), *Epodes* II.34 and Martial XIII.92. Bile and phlegm were two of the humours (phlegm, black bile, yellow bile and blood) and Horace is here imitating the language of medicine (see OCD s.v. 'humours', where it is stated that 'the Hippocratic author of *Affections* proposes that bile and phlegm are principal fluids involved in disease'). Horace is not expecting medical knowledge here: the simple contrast is made between 'sweet' (**dulcia**) and the bitter **bilem** followed by the political metaphor **tumultum** ('rioting') in the stomach and the expressive description of the 'slow' phlegm. **pītuītă** is scanned as three syllables by synizesis with the central *-ui-* scanned as a diphthong. For the runny nose as a sign of ill-health see *Epistles* I.1.108, Catullus XXIII.17.

76–7 Everyone (**omnis**) gets up pale in complexion (**pallidus**) from a 'spoilt for choice' dinner. The **cena ... dubia** was a joke coined by Terence *Phormio* 342 where the 'dubious' dinner is one where you are dubious what to eat first because there is a confusing variety of dishes, although Horace is giving a more negative view of such a meal and may be quoting the popular term ironically. Paleness often indicates sickness – see the *pallentes morbi* in Virgil's underworld (*Aeneid* VI.275), Juvenal 10.189.

77–9 quin ('what's more') introduces a further thought to explain the previous lines. The gourmand's body is weighed down (**onustum**) with 'yesterday's excesses' (the abstract **vitiis** standing for the concrete foods, as at 21 above). For the image see Juvenal I.142–3 ('you carry an undigested peacock into the baths'). The heavy undigested meal of the previous day 'weighs down the heart along with itself (**una**) and nails to the earth the particle of divine breath'. The Stoics and Pythagoreans believed that the human soul was made up of the same divine fiery ether which exists above the sky and that the wise man would seek to join his small part of this divine ether to the rest of the godhead. That which was fiery and airy was light and divine, as opposed to the wet and the earthy which keep us from achieving our divine goal. It may be that the poet is here mocking (with their own terminology) the hypocrisy of people who preach austerity (often in Stoic terms) but whose lifestyle is likely to defeat their aspirations.

80–1 The wise man who eats sparingly is quick to return to work after sleep. **dicto citius** ('more quickly than said') is common in epic and in prose (cf. Virgil *Aeneid* I.142, Petronius 74) as a lively descriptive phrase and goes here with both the refreshment and the sleeping. **curata** agrees with **membra** and indicates food, drink and washing (cf. *Odes* III.17.15, Virgil *Georgics* IV.187, Lucretius II.31). **sopori** is dative with **dedit** ('gave their refreshed limbs over to sleep'). The instant rising is brought out by the strong adjective **vegetus** ('vigorous') and the present tense **surgit** balancing **sopori** in the same position in the previous line.

82–8 The man who overeats all the time risks damaging his health and soon stops enjoying the rich foods he eats: but the man of austere diet may treat himself occasionally and give himself more pleasure in doing so, as Epicurus did (see note on line 1).

82 The image of **transcurrere** is that of lithe running from one mode of being to another and well suits the nimble healthy eater as opposed to the greedy man weighed down in 77–8: **melius** means 'a better diet' but does not imply that the *victus tenuis* ('simple life') is worse than other diets, while **quondam** means 'now and then' to remind us not to make a habit of such treats.

83–4 sive … seu … mean 'whether … or whether …'. The subject of **advexerit** is the 'returning year' bringing a 'feast day'. Such feast days were often anniversaries such as birthdays (*Odes* IV.11, Persius 2, Juvenal XII.1–3) or anniversaries of other events personal (e.g. *Odes* III.8) or political (2 September, for example, was declared a *dies festus* as it was the anniversary of the battle of Actium) or religious, where sacrifice might well give people a rare taste of roast meat.

84 If the *victus tenuis* has made a body unduly thin (**tenuatum**) then richer food will 'restore' it. This contrasts with the man who is **pinguem vitiis** (21) who gorges every day. The image of the wise man

as one who practises asceticism and so is likely to be thin recalls the
avoidance of luxuries common to Cynicism and Epicureanism and
the later figure of the philosopher Seneca (Tacitus *Annals* XV.63).

85–6 Old age commonly brings loss of weight and renders a man
weak (**imbecilla**). Here the poet transfers the agencies involved: it is
the years which 'mount up' and the 'age' (**aetas**) which wishes to be
treated more gently (**mollius**), the passive infinitive **tractari** helping
to reinforce the point that the old man now is helpless in the hands of
others. For the pathetic weakness of the aged see Juvenal X.190–288.

86–8 mollius in 85 is picked up in **mollitiem** in 87, and **accedent**
(85) gives us **accedet** (86), just as **validus** (87) looks back to **vegetus**
(81) and forward to **valetudo** (88). The argument runs thus: if you
are already (**prae-**) adopting the feebleness of old age while you are
a healthy boy, then what on earth (**quidnam**) will be added to that
feebleness if ill-health or sluggish old age hit you? The contrast is
heavily drawn between young (**puer**) and old (**senectus**), healthy
(**validus**) and unhealthy (**dura valetudo**) and the satirist is once again
pointing out the topsy-turvy world in which the young act as if they
were old and 'feebleness' is imagined as a resource for old age which
the young are using prematurely.

89–93 The thinking is as follows: in old days men praised the boar
which had gone off – not because they did not mind the smell, but
because they approved of the master having the self-control to forgo
the fresh meat in case a guest turned up later on. In other words,
hospitality towards strangers was a stronger impulse than the desire
for fresh meat. The thought reminds us of Cicero's sneer at the
Epicurean Piso for eating rotten meat (*in Pisonem* 67).

89–92 The opening words are shocking and amount to a *reductio
ad absurdum*. The men of old did not praise rotting meat per se

(which would only be possible if they had no nose at all) – they praised the virtues which allowed meat to go off rather than risk denying hospitality. **hac mente** means 'with this intention' (cf. I.1.30). **commodius** must here mean something like 'more obligingly' (as at *Epistles* I.9.9). The kind host will save the meat for a potential guest until it has gone off – unlike the **edax** ('greedy-guts') master who eats it **integrum** – which means both 'fresh' and also 'whole'.

92–3 The ironic hyperbole of this exclamation makes it likely that the preceding few lines are ironic. The key word **heroas** is stressed by the enjambement and its initial position in the line; and the language of the phrase ('if only the early earth had brought me forth, born amid these heroes!') suggests the myth of the primordial *gegeneis* or 'earth-born' who sprang from the earth already armed and grown: see I.3.99 and cf. the myth of the Thebans born from the earth after Cadmus sowed the dragon's teeth (Ovid *Metamorphoses* III.95–130: more rationalist versions of the story existed such as Lucretius V.783–836). The epic language and the elegant phrasing of 93 – after the more colloquial and prosaic register of 89–92 – strikes an ironic note of mockery of such 'golden age' rhetoric.

94–111 The poet has so far concentrated on the personal reasons for the simple life (*victus tenuis*). He now turns to the social and political benefits.

94–5 das aliquid famae has the sense 'you grant some importance to reputation'. *fama* was of massive importance both to the person whose reputation was under discussion (see most famously Virgil *Aeneid* IV.173–97) and to the rest of society eager to hear the latest gossip, and both senses are available here: hearing good things about oneself (or news about others) is 'more pleasing than song' and certainly 'occupies the ear'. The subjunctive **occupet** is causal – *fama* is important to him 'insofar as it takes hold of the ear' (a phrase also

found in Virgil *Aeneid* III.294). *fama* would not matter if nobody took
any notice of it.

95–9 The negative sort of *fama* is here presented in the picture of the
big spender who earns all the bad effects of his habits. The language
here is rhetorical: notice the anaphora of **grandes ... grande** (with
the second of these promoted in enjambement), the alliterative
juxtaposition of the two key words **damno dedecus**, the didactic
imperative **adde** and the asyndeton of the list of personal enemies
you will make.

95 The *rhombus* was the turbot, the monster fish immortalized in
Juvenal *Satire* 4 and a byword for luxury food: see I.2.115–16, *Epode*
II.50, Persius VI.23, Juvenal XI.120–1. Horace has already singled it
out as the fish which is too big to be eaten fresh earlier in this poem
(42). The **patinae** are 'dishes' in general rather than a specific fish-
kettle or the like: in *Epistles* 1.15.34 it is a plate of ox-tripe.

96 The double loss of money (**damno**) and reputation (**dedecus**) is
reminiscent of the hapless spendthrift lover in Lucretius IV.1123–40;
and the prodigal spender is mocked at Juvenal XI.2–5.

97 The prodigal earns the anger of his uncle, his neighbours and
then himself as he finally realizes his folly, with the three 'enemies'
juxtaposed in asyndeton to make a threatening trio. The uncle on the
father's side had some share in the responsibility for keeping the family
fortune intact – unlike the more indulgent grandfather or maternal
uncle – and was commonly seen as censorious (cf. II.3.88, *Odes* III.12.3,
Catullus 74.1, Persius I.11). For the scorn of neighbours see 1.1.85.

98–9 Self-disgust may lead to suicide, as in the case of Ajax who
committed suicide after his madness when he had been mocked by
his fellow Greeks (the story is dramatized in Sophocles' *Ajax*); and

this sombre thought becomes a sick joke here as the wretched man longs for death 'in vain' (**frustra**) as he does not even have a penny (**as**) to buy himself a noose (**laquei**).

99–100 The poet's companion replies that such words of warning do not apply to him as he is wealthy: he therefore has the means to support his extravagant lifestyle and will not be reduced to a comic and/or suicidal figure. **iure** means 'deservedly': *iurgo* has already been used in this poem (22) as 'scold' or 'criticize'. **Trausius** is a Roman name but this man is not known.

100–1 The man's wealth is conveyed in suitably expansive terms with the double phrase **vectigalia magna divitiasque** describing his 'great revenues and riches' and then by describing the riches hyperbolically as 'sufficiently big for three kings'. Kings were a symbol of fortune, wealth and arbitrary spending: cf. *Odes* II.12.21, III.9.4, Virgil *Georgics* IV.132.

102 quod superat ('that which is left over' – i.e. 'the surplus wealth', understanding a word like *id* as antecedent for **quod**) is the object of **insumere**: 'is there then (**ergo** line 101) nothing better to spend your surplus wealth on?'

103–5 A tricolon of indignant questions addressed to the rich man, each beginning with a word denoting 'why?' (**cur ... quare ... cur ...**). The point being made – that the rich have a duty to pay towards the general good of poorer folk – is unusual in satire which more commonly speaks from the point of view of the underdog lamenting the unfairness of it all rather than appealing to a social conscience.

103 The concepts of poverty (**eget**) and of riches (**divite**) frame the question, with **te divite** in the ablative absolute construction ('while you are rich'). The word **indignus** is loaded: if a man is poor owing to his own folly or vice then there is (it is implied) no moral reason to help him, as in the modern distinction between the 'deserving' and the 'undeserving poor'.

104 The money could be donated to the repair of crumbling temples. This was topical in an age in which the new emperor Augustus would later claim to have restored eighty-two temples of the gods (*Res Gestae* XX.4, Suetonius *Augustus* 29: see Horace *Odes* II.15.20, III.6.2–4). **deum** is genitive plural (shortened from *deorum*).

104–5 The final question is the angriest of the three: after care of the individual and worship of the gods, the poet turns to the 'beloved fatherland' (**carae … patriae**) and asks the rich man to 'measure out something' from 'so massive a heap'. For the image of the heap of money cf. I.1.44, I.1.51. The moral outrage is explicit in the vocative **improbe** ('heartless scoundrel': the word connotes greed and amoral acquisitiveness as at Virgil *Georgics* I.119 and *Aeneid* IV.386) and implicit both in the adjectives **carae** and **tanto** and in the use of the emotive word **patriae. emetiris** assumes that the man has an amount of money which is more easily weighed than counted, like the rich man in I.1.96 and later on Trimalchio's wife Fortunata who 'measures her cash by the bushel' (Petronius 37).

106 Heavy sarcasm. 'You alone of course (**nimirum**) will always have a prosperous lifestyle.' The point is that one cannot guarantee that present-day success will continue into the future and you may find that you will need others one day. *recte esse* is colloquial Latin for 'to be OK' and **res** here means 'wealth' (OLD s.v. 'res' 1).

107–8 The miser will make enemies – cf. V.1.66–7 – who will laugh at his later (**posthac**) downfall. The *-ne* in **uterne** is superfluous. The language is expressive: 'which of these two will trust in himself with more self-confidence when facing uncertain outcomes?' **casus**

dubios is also something of a tautology as *casus* ('accident, chance') is by its very nature 'uncertain' and both nicely contrast with the solid sureness of **certius.**

109 The man of epicene tastes is sketched as one who 'has accustomed his scornful mind and body to having more (than he needs)'. **pluribus** is contrasted with **parvo** in 110, and the adjective **superbum** reminds us of the rich man's selfish disdain for others in lines 103–7.

110 contentus parvo is an Epicurean stock theme (Lucretius V.1118–19) and a common theme in poetry of this period, as in *Epistles* I.10.41, II.1.139, *Odes* II.11.5, II.16.13, Tibullus I.1.25. Above all, the return to the theme of the opening of this poem, as he begins to round off the composition, is a good piece of ring-composition, which helps to convey the coherence and the thematic control at work in poetry such as this which also cultivates the appearance of improvised rhapsodic utterance. **metuens … futuri** ('anxious about the future') indicates a healthy prudence – like that of the ant in I.1.35 – rather than an obsessive neurosis, as is made clear in the military imagery of the next line.

111 The line is neatly framed by peace and war, with the subject given the approving gloss of **sapiens** who, like the ant in *Satire* I.1, has kitted himself out for war while the state is at peace and so will be ready when the enemy strikes.

112–36: The poem concludes with a sketch (112–25) of the contented countryman Ofellus practising what he preaches; and a final note (126–36) on the mutability of fortune and the way we possess nothing for long, in the wake of the recent land-expulsions. 'Live brave lives and hold out brave hearts against adversity' is the rousing conclusion of this wonderful poem.

Vocabulary

An asterisk * denotes a word in OCR's Defined Vocabulary List for AS.

This vocabulary lists every word in the text. Nouns are listed with their genitive singular, and verbs are listed with all their four principal parts. Adjectives are listed with the endings of the different genders (e.g. **bonus -a -um**) except where the three genders are the same in the nominative where the genitive is listed (e.g. **iners, inertis**).

*a, ab (+ablative)	from out of
abnormis -e	irregular (II.2.3)
abortivus -a -um	prematurely born
*ac	and
accedo, accedere, accessi, accessum	to mount up, be added
*accipio, accipere, accepi, acceptum	to obtain, to take in (II.2.70)
acclinis -e (+ dative)	inclined towards
*acer, acris, acre	fierce (I.1.58), forceful (I.3.53)
acervus -i, m	heap
*acies, aciei, f	vision, eyesight
acutus -a -um	sharp
*ad (+accusative)	to, when facing (II.2.108)
*adde	(*imperative of addo*) throw in
*addo, addere, addidi, additum	to add
adfero, adferre, attuli, allatum	to bring
adfigo, adfigere, adfixi, adfixum	to pin down, attach
adsideo, adsidere, adsedi, adsessum	to sit by one's side
adsuetus -a -um	accustomed
*adsum, adesse, adfui	to be present, to exist

adveho, advehere, advexi, advectum	to bring
***advĕnio, advenire, advēni, adventum**	to arrive
adusque + accusative	right up to
	(= *usque ad*)
***aequus -a -um**	fair, just, reasonable
āer, āeris, m	the upper air
aestus -ūs, m	summer heat
aetas, aetatis, f	age, time of life
***ager, agri**, m	field
***ago, agere, ēgi, actum**	to stir into action (II.2.13)
agricola -ae, m	farmer
ait	he says
albus -a -um	pale, white
***aliquis, aliqua, aliquid**	somebody, something
***alius, alia, aliud**	other, another
***alter, altera, alterum**	another man, somebody else
amator, amatoris, m	lover
***amica -ae**, f	girlfriend
amicitia -ae, f	friendship
***amicus -i**, m	friend
***amitto, amittere, amisi, amissum**	to lose
***amo, amare, amavi, amatum**	to love
***amor, amoris**, m	affection, love
amplius (adverb)	more
amplus -a -um	more than enough (II.2.101)
***an**	or
***animus -i**, m	mind, soul
***annus -i**, m	year
***ante**	earlier (*adverbial*: I.1.37)
antiquus -a -um	ancient
aper, apri, m	boar

apertus -a -um	open to attack, exposed
appello, appellare, appellavi, appellatum	to call, name
apto, aptare, aptavi, aptatum	to fasten on, fit
aptus -a -um	suited
***aqua -ae**, f	water
Aquarius	Aquarius (the constellation: I.1.36)
***aquila -ae**, f	eagle
aratrum -i, n	plough
arca -ae, f	money-chest
area -ae, f	threshing-floor
***argentum -i**, n	silver (I.1.41), money (I.1.86)
aro, arare, aravi, aratum	to plough
as, assis, m	penny
asellus -i, m	donkey
astutus -a -um	cunning, sly
***at**	but
āter, ātra, ātrum	black, dark
Athenae -arum, f	Athens (*locative case* **Athenis** 'in Athens')
atque	and
attineo, attinere, attinui, attentum	to be relevant (II.2.27)
***audax, audacis**	reckless
Aufidus -i, m	Aufidus (a river in Venusia: I.1.58)
aura -ae, f	breath, air
auris -is, f	ear
aurum -i, n	gold
Auster –tri, m	the south wind
austerus -a -um	harsh
***aut** or (**aut … aut**	… = 'either … or …')

avello, avellere, avelli/avulsi, avulsum	to tear off, pull away
aveo, avere	to desire
avis -is, f	bird
Balbinus -i, m	Balbinus (I.3.40)
balbutio, balbutire	to stammer
***bellum -i**, n	war
***bene** (adverb from *bonus*)	well
***bibo, bibere, bibi**	to drink
bilis -is, f	bile
***bonus -a -um**	good
caecus -a -um	blind
calceus -i, m	sandal, shoe
caldior (= *calidior*)	hot-headed
Campus -i, m	The Campus Martius (I.1.91)
cantus -ūs, m	singing
***capio, capere, cepi, captum**	hold (I.3.46)
capto, captare, captavi, captatum	snatch at, grasp after
careo, carere, carui, caritum	(+ ablative) to lack
carmen, carminis, n	song
caro, carnis, f	meat
***carus -a -um**	dear, beloved
casus -ūs, m	misfortune (I.1.81), accident, chance event (II.2.108)
cauda -ae, f	tail
caupo, cauponis, m	innkeeper
cedens, cedentis	yielding, unresisting
***cena -ae**, f	dinner
***centum**	100
***cerno, cernere, crevi, cretum**	to see

*certius (comparative adverb from *certus*)	more confidently
cibarius -a -um	rationed (food: I.1.32)
*cibus -i, m	food
citus -a -um	quick, swift
*clamo, clamare, clamavi, clamatum	to proclaim
coctus -a -um	cooked
*cogo, cogere, coegi, coactum	to compel
cognatus -a -um	relative, kin
cognomen, cognominis, n	descriptive name
comminuo, comminuere, comminui, comminutum	to reduce
commodius (comparative adverb from *commodus*)	more obligingly
communis sensus, communis sensūs	fellow-feeling (I.3.66)
compenso, compensare, compensavi, compensatum	to weigh up
compilo, compilare, compilavi, compilatum	to fleece (I.1.78), rob
conchylium -ii, n	shellfish
concinnus -a -um	sociable, good company
concurritur (from *concurro*)	battle is joined (I.1.7)
concutio, concutere, concussi, concussum	to shake
condolesco, condolescere, condolui	to be in pain
congero, congerere, congessi, congestum	to heap up
construo, construere, construxi, constructum	to pile up
consuetudo, consuetudinis, f	habit
consultor -oris, m	legal client

consumo, consumere, consumpsi, consumptum	to eat
contemno, contemnere, contempsi, contemptum	to despise
contemplor, contemplari, contemplatus sum	to gaze on
contentus -a -um	satisfied, content
*contra (*adverbial*)	on the other hand
contristo, contristare, contristavi, contristatum	to sadden
copia -ae, f	supply
*corpus, corporis, n	body
corrumpo, corrumpere, corrupi, corruptum	to bribe (II.2.9), seduce (II.2.25)
crassus -a -um	coarse (II.2.3)
*credo, credere, credidi, creditum	to believe
*crimen, criminis, n	allegation, accusation
crus, cruris, n	leg
*cum (+ ablative)	with
*cum (conjunction)	when, since, although
cumera -ae, f	bread-basket
cupido, cupidinis, m/f	desire
*cupidus -a -um (+ genitive)	eager for
*cupio, cupire, cupi(v)i, cupitum	to want
*cur	why
*curo, curare, curavi, curatum	to refresh
*curro, currere, cucurri, cursum	to run
cyathus -i, m	ladle
damnum -i, n	financial loss

*de (+ ablative)	from (I.1.55), about (I.1.69)
*debeo, debere, debui, debitum	to be obliged to
*decipio, decipere, decepi, deceptum	to deceive
dedecus, dedecoris, n	disgrace
*defendo, defendere, defendi, defensum	to protect
defluo, defluere, defluxi, defluxum	to hang loosely (I.3.31)
demissus -a -um	humble, unassuming
defodio, defodere, defōdi, defossum	to dig out
delecto, delectare, delectavi, delectatum	to please, delight
demŏveo, demovere, demōvi, demotum	to divert, distract
*denique	in short, to summarize (I.1.92)
depono, deponere, deposui, depositum	to bury, deposit
desum, deesse, defui (+ dative)	to be lacking
desurgo, desurgere, desurrexi, desurrectum	to get up from
*deus -i, m	god
*dico, dicere, dixi, dictum (imperative: dic)	to say
*dies, diei, m	day
diluo, diluere, dilui, dilutum	to water down, mix with
*disco, discere, didici	to learn, be informed of
discus -i, m	discus
disquiro, disquirere	to investigate, discuss
disto, distare	to be different
distortus -a -um	deformed, twisted
*ditior	= *divitior* (comparative of **dives**)
diversus -a -um	different
*dives, divitis	rich
divido, dividere, dīvīsi, divisum	to cut down the middle

divinus -a -um	divine
*__divitiae__ -arum, f.pl.**	wealth, riches
*__do, dare, dedi, datum__**	to give
*__doceo, docere, docui, doctum__**	to teach
*__doleo, dolere, dolui, dolitum__**	to suffer pain, grieve
*__domi__ (locative of *domus*)**	at home
*__dominus -i__, m**	master (of the house)
*__dubius -a -um__**	uncertain
dulcis -e	sweet
*__dum__**	so long as (I.1.40), provided that (I.1.52)
*__durus -a -um__**	hard (I.1.28), harsh (II.2.88)
edax edacis	gluttonous, greedy
*__egeo__ (+ genitive)**	to want, have need of
*__ego__ (pronoun)**	1
eheu	alas!
elixus -a -um	boiled
emetior, emetiri, emensus sum	to measure out
*__emo, emere, emi, emptum__**	to buy
*__enim__**	see **quid enim?**
*__eo__**	to such a point (I.1.56), for that reason (I.3.30)
Epidaurius -a -um	Epidaurian (I.3.27)
*__equus -i__, m**	horse
*__ergo__ (adverb)**	then, in that case
eripio, eripere, eripui, ereptum	to rescue from (+ *quin* II.2.23)
*__erro, errare, erravi, erratum__**	to make a mistake
error, erroris, m	mistake, error
esca -ae, f	food
esto	'let it be so', 'very well then' (II.2.30)
*__et__**	and

*etiam	also, even
evenio, evenire, eveni, eventum	to turn out, occur
*ex (+ ablative)	from out of
examino, examinare, examinavi, examinatum	to weigh up (the evidence)
exanimis -e	faint, lifeless
*exemplum -i, n	example
extraho, extrahere, extraxi, extractum	to drag out of
extundo, extundere, extudi, extusum	to hammer out
fabula -ae, f	story
*facio, facere, feci, factum	to do, act
Falernum -i, n	Falernian wine
*fallo, fallere, fefelli, falsum	to trick, deceive
falsus -a -um	false, fake
*fama -ae, f	reputation
fastidio, fastidire, fastidi(v)i, fastiditum	to feel revulsion towards
fastidium -i, n	fussiness, fastidiousness
fatigo, fatigare, fatigavi, fatigatum	to tire, exhaust
*felix, felicis	fortunate
*fero, ferre, tuli, latum	to bear (I.1.31, II.2.93), carry off (I.1.58), bring (II.2.76, II.2.96)
*ferrum -i, n	(iron) sword (I.1.39)
fervidus -a -um	boiling
festus -a -um	festival, feast (day)
fictus -a -um	false, sham, hypocritical
*fido, fidere, fisus sum	(+ dative) to trust
*filius -(i)i, m	son
filix, filicis, f	fern, bracken
finio, finire, fini(v)i, finitum	to put an end to

*finis -is, m	boundary, limit
*fio, fieri, factus sum	to happen
*flumen, fluminis, n	river
fomentum -i, n	remedy (I.1.82)
fonticulus -i, m	small spring
foris (adverb)	out of the house
forma -ae, f	appearance
formica -ae, f	ant
formido, formidare, formidavi, formidatum	to fear
fors, fortis	chance
*forte (adverb)	by chance, perhaps
*fortis -e	strong
fortunatus -a -um	fortunate
*frango, frangere, fregi, fractum	to break
frenum -i, n	bridle, reins
*frigus, frigoris, n	cold
frugi	(indeclinable adjective) sensible, honest
*frumentum -i, n	grain
*frustra (adverb)	in vain
*fugio, fugere, fūgi	to run away, flee
fulcio, fulcire, fulsi, fultum	to support
fulgor, fulgoris, m	shining, brightness
fur, furis, m	thief
furtim (adverb)	stealthily
futurus -a -um (future participle from *sum*)	future
gallina -ae, f	chicken
gallus -i, m	cock
*gaudeo, gaudere, gavisus sum	to take pleasure in
*genus, generis, n	type, kind

gnatus -i, m (= *natus*)	son
graecor, graecari	to act like a Greek
granarium -i, n	granary
grandis -e	large, great
gratus -a -um	pleasing
***gravis -e**	heavy
***habeo, habere, habui, habitum**	to have, own, consider (I.3.52)
haereo, haerere, haesi, haesum	to stick, be fastened
Hagna -ae, f	Hagna (I.3.40)
***haud**	not
haurio, haurire, hausi, haustum	to draw off, take
heros, heroos, m	hero
hesternus -a -um	of yesterday
***hic, haec, hoc**	this
***hīc** (adverb)	here
hiemo, hiemare, hiemavi, hiematum	to be stormy
***hiems, hiemis**, f	winter
holus, holeris, n	vegetables
***homo, hominis**, m	man, person
honestus -a -um	honourable
***honor, honoris**, m	distinction
***hora -ae**, f	hour
***hospes, hospitis**, m	guest, visitor
humanus -a -um	human
***humus -i**, f	earth, ground
Hymetius -a -um	from Mt Hymettus (II.2.15)
iactans, iactantis (*comparative iactantior*)	boastful
iacto, iactare, iactavi, iactatum	to toss, throw about
***iam**	by now, already
***idem, eadem, idem**	the same

*idoneus -a -um	fit, suitable, appropriate
ignarus -a -um	ignorant of (+ genitive)
*ignis -is, m	fire
ignosco, ignoscere, ignovi, ignotum	
(+ dative)	that
*ille, illa, illud	to pardon
*illuc (adverb)	to that place/fact (I.3.38)
imbecillus -a -um	weak
immensus -a -um	immense, huge
impar, imparis	unequal, differing
impello, impellere, impuli, impulsum	to disturb
impransus -a -um	having not had lunch
imprimis (adverb)	first and foremost
improbus -a -um	shameless, heartless
*in (+ ablative)	in
*in (+ accusative)	into, against
inanis -e	empty, hungry
incautus -a -um	without thought (for)
*incendium -i, n	fire
incido, incidere, incidi, incasum	to strike, occur
*incipio, incipere, incepi, inceptum	to begin
inclino, inclinare, inclinavi,	
inclinatum	to tip the scales (I.3.71)
incrusto, incrustare, incrustavi,	
incrustatum	to stain
incultus -a -um	uncultivated, uncouth
indignus -a -um	undeserving
indomitus -a -um	untamed, uncontrolled
indormio, indormire, indormi(v)i	
(+ dative)	to fall asleep over
ineptus -a -um	silly, inappropriate
infelix, infelicis	unsuccessful

*ingenium -i, n	talent
*ingens, ingentis	huge, massive
inhio, inhiare, inhiavi, inhiatum	to be open-mouthed, to gape
*inimicus -i, m	enemy
*iniquus -a -um	hostile, ill-disposed towards
innascor, innasci, innatus sum	to grow in
*inquimus (from *inquam* (irregular verb))	we say
inquiro, inquirere, inquisi(v)i, inquisitum	to inquire into
*inquit (from *inquam*)	he says
insanus -a -um	crazy, senseless
insero, inserere, insevi, insitum	to sow
*insidiae -arum, f.pl.	trap, ambush
insumo, insumere, insumpsi, insumptum	to spend
integer, integra, integrum	whole, fresh (II.2.92)
*inter (+ accusative)	amongst
*intra (+ accusative)	within
inunguo, inunguere, inunxi, inunctum	to smear with ointment
inverto, invertere, inverti, inversum	to turn inside out, to reverse
invidia -ae, f	resentment
*ipse, ipsa, ipsum	-self, himself, themselves
iracundus -a -um (comparative iracundior)	irascible, prone to anger
*iratus -a -um	angry
*is, ea, id	he, she, it
*iste, ista, istud	that
*ita ... ut ...	to such an extent ... that ...

*iubeo, iubere, iussi, iussum	to tell, order
*iudex, iudicis, m	judge
iugerum -i, n	two-thirds of an acre of land
*iungo, iungere, iunxi, iunctum	to join, unite
iure (ablative of ius used adverbially)	rightly
iurgo, iurgare, iurgavi, iurgatum	to scold, rebuke
ius, iuris, n	law-code
*iustus -a -um	right
iuvo, iuvare, iuvi, iutum	to benefit, delight
*labor, laboris, m	effort, hard work
labrum -i, n	lip
*laetus -a -um	joyful
lagois, lagoidis, f	rock ptarmigan
lanx, lancis, f	dish, dinner-plate
laqueus -i, m	noose
lassus -a -um	tired
lateo, latere, latui	to lie hidden
latro, latrare, latravi, latratum	to growl, rumble
*latus, lateris, n	side, flank
*laudo, laudare, laudavi, laudatum	to praise
laxus -a -um	loose
lectus -i, m	bed
*lego, legere, legi, lectum	to read
lenio, lenire, lenivi, lenitum	to ease, soothe
*lentus -a -um	slow, sluggish
lepus, leporis, m	hare
*lex, legis, f	law
*libenter (adverb)	willingly, gladly
*liber, libera, liberum	outspoken
liberta -ae, f	freedwoman
limus -i, m	mud
lippus -a -um	suffering an eye-infection

liquidus -a -um	liquid
***longus -a -um**	long
lucrum -i, n	gain, profit
Maecenas, Maecenatis, m	Maecenas (I.1.1)
***magis** (+ ablative)	more (than)
***magnus -a -um**	large, great, big
***mala, malorum**, n.pl. (from **malus**)	faults (I.3.25)
***male** (adverb from **malus**)	badly
***malo, malle, malui**	to prefer
***malus -a -um**	bad, evil
***mare, maris**, n	sea
***mecum**	with me
medicus -i, m	doctor
***medius -a -um**	(down the) middle (I.1.100)
mel, mellis, n	honey
***melior, melius** (comparative of **bonus**)	better
***melius** (adverb from **melior**)	better
membrum -i, n	limb
memor, memoris	mindful of, remembering
memoro, memorare, memoravi, memoratum	to make mention of
***mens, mentis**, f	mind, intention
mensa -ae, f	table
***mercator -oris**, m	merchant
mereor, mereri, meritus sum	to deserve
metior, metiri, mensus sum	to weigh out, measure
metuo, metuere, metui, metutum	to fear
***metus -ūs**, m	fear
***meus -a -um**	my
***miles, militis**, m	soldier
militia -ae, f	military service

*mille (plural: milia)	thousand
Minerva -ae, f	Minerva (II.2.3)
*minimus -a -um (superlative of parvus)	smallest
*minus (adverb)	less
*miror, mirari, miratus sum	to be surprised
misceo, miscere, miscui, mixtum	to mix together
*miser, misera, miserum	miserable
*modo	see si modo
molestus -a -um	unwelcome, troublesome
mollis -e	soft, gentle
mollities -ei, f	softness
momentum -i, n	crisis, turning-point
*mors, mortis, f	death
*multo (adverb)	much
*multum (adverb)	very much
munia, munium, n.pl.	duties, tasks
*muto, mutare, mutavi, mutatum	to change
*nam	for
naris -is, f	nose
*narro, narrare, narravi, narratum	to tell a story
*nascor, nasci, natus sum	to be born
nasus -i, m	nose, sense of smell
*natura -ae, f	nature
*nauta -ae, m	sailor
*navis -is, f	ship
*ne (+ subjunctive)	so that … not (I.1.94), do not (II.2.16)
*nec	nor
*neglego, neglegere, neglexi, neglectum	to neglect
*nego, negare, negavi, negatum	to deny, refuse
*nemo	nobody
*neque … neque/nec	neither … nor …

*nescio, nescire, nescivi	not to know
*ni (= nisi)	unless
nidor -oris, m	aroma
*nihil	nothing
*nil	nothing
nimirum	of course
*nisi	unless
nitens, nitentis	shining, gleaming
*nobiscum	with us
*noceo, nocere, nocui, nocitum	to harm
*nomen, nominis, n	name
*non	not
*nos	we, us
nosmet	ourselves
*noster, nostra, nostrum	our
*notus -a -um	acquainted
*nox, noctis, f	night
*nullus -a -um	not any, no
*num	(to see) whether (I.3.35)
*num?	surely not?
numero, numerare, numeravi, numeratum	to count
nummus -i, m	money, cash
*nunc	now
o	oh!
obdo, obdere, obdidi, obditum	to expose
obicio, obicere, obieci, obiectum	to throw in someone's way
obsto, obstare, obstiti, obstatum	to stand in the way of, block
*occupo, occupare, occupavi, occupatum	to occupy, seize hold of
*oculus -i, m	eye

***odi, odisse** (defective verb)	to hate
Ofellus -i, m	Ofellus (II.2.2)
offendo, offendere, offendi, offensum	to offend, displease
***offero, offerre, obtuli, oblatum**	to present
***olim**	in earlier days, formerly
***omnis -e**	all, everybody
onustus -a -um	loaded down
***opera -ae**, f	effort
opinor, opinari, opinatus sum	to think, believe
***opprimo, opprimere, oppressi,**	
oppressum	to crush, overwhelm
***optimus -a -um**	best
opto, optare, optavi, optatum	to wish
***opus esse**	to have need of (I.1.54)
***os, oris**, n	mouth
ostium -i, n	door
ostrea -ae, f	oyster
***otium -i**, n	leisure, retirement
paetus -a -um	having a cast in the eye
palatum -i, n	palate
pallidus -a -um	pale
pandat, pandere, pandi, pansum	to spread out, unfold
panis -is, m	bread
***parco, parcere, peperci**	to spare, refrain from using
parcus -a -um	parsimonious, thrifty
***pareo, parere, parui, paritum** (+ dative)	to obey
***pario, parere, peperi, partum**	to produce (I.1.94)
***paro, parare, paravi, paratum**	to prepare
***pars, partis**, f	proportion, part
particula -ae, f	particle

parvulus -a -um	tiny (diminutive of **parvus**)
*parvus -a -um	small, little
*pater, patris, m	father
patina -ae, f	dish
*patria -ae, f	fatherland
patruus -i, m	uncle (father's brother)
*paulo (adverb)	a little bit
*pauper, pauperis	poor
pauperies -ei, f	poverty
pavo, pavonis, m	peacock
*pax, pacis, f	peace
peccatum -i, n	failing, misdemeanour
penuria -ae, f	shortage
*per (+ accusative)	through, across
*perdo, perdere, perdidi, perditum	to waste
peregrinus -a -um	foreign
perfidus -a -um	cheating
*peritus -a -um (+ genitive)	expert in
pervideo, pervidere, pervidi, pervisum	to see
*pes, pedis, m	foot
*peto, petere, petivi, petitum	to make for, seek out
pictus -a -um	painted, coloured
pila -ae, f	ball
pinguis -e	thick (I.3.58), fat (II.2.21)
piscis -is, m	fish
pituita -ae, f	phlegm
plane (adverb)	clearly
plaudo, plaudere, plausi, plausum	to applaud
*plenus -a -um	plentiful
pluma -ae, f	plumage, feather
*plures -a	more

*plus (adverb)	more
polypus -i, m	nasal polyp/tumour
*pono, ponere, posui, positum	to place, apply (I.3.42), serve (II.2.23)
pondus, ponderis, n	weight
*populus -i, m	people
*porto, portare, portavi, portatum	to carry
*posco, poscere, poposci	to ask for
*possum, posse, potui	to be able
*post (+ accusative)	after
posthac (adverb)	afterwards, later on
*postulo, postulare, postulavi, postulatum	to demand, require
*potior, potius	preferable
*potius (adverb)	in preference
*praebeo, praebere, praebui, praebitum	to offer, provide
praecipio, praecipere, praecepi, praeceptum	to teach
praegravo, praegravare, praegravavi, praegravatum	to weigh down
praescribo, praescribere, praescripsi, praescriptum	to prescribe
praesto, praestare, praestiti, praestatum	to offer
praesumo, praesumere, praesumpsi, praesumptum	to make early use of
praevertor, praeverti, praeversus sum	to turn one's attention towards
pravus -a -um	bent, crooked
*pretium -i, n	price, cost
*primus -a -um	early (II.2.93)
*pro (+ ablative)	instead of (I.3.61)
probus -a -um	decent

promus -i, m	steward
propinquus -i, m	kinsman, relative
proprius -a -um	one's own
prorepo, prorepere, prorepsi, proreptum	to creep out
***puella -ae**, f	girl
***puer, pueri**, m	boy
pulcher, pulchra, pulchrum	beautiful, attractive
pullus -i, m	chick
pulmentarium -i, n	relish, sauce
pulso, pulsare, pulsavi, pulsatum	to batter, beat
***puto, putare, putavi, putatum**	to think
qua = quae	(I.3.35)
***quaero, quaerere, quaesivi, quaesitum**	to look for, seek out
***qualis -e**	the sort of
***quam**	than, as (I.3.27), how! (I.3.67)
quamvis	although
***quantus -a -um**	how much, how great
quare	why
quatenus	since, insofar as
***qui, quae, quod**	who, what
***quia**	because
***quid?**	what?, why? (I.1.69)
quid enim?	'Of course!', 'It goes without saying'
***quidam, quaedam, quoddam**	a certain person, somebody
quidquam	anything
quin	but that (II.2.23), what's more (II.2.77)
quis	= **quibus** (II.1.75)
quis, quid	somebody, something

*quisquam, quicquam	anyone
quivis, quaevis, quodvis	some … or other
*quo	for what purpose? (I.1.73)
*quod	because (I.3.30), the fact that (I.3.38)
quodcumque	whatever
quondam	now and then, on occasions
*quoque	also
rancidus -a -um	rank, rotting
rarus -a -um	rare
*ratio, rationis, f	rational choice, reasoning
recedo, recedere, recessi, recessum	to retire
recreo, recreare, recreavi, recreatum	to restore
recte esse	to be well
recuso, recusare, recusavi, recusatum	to reject, refuse
*reddo, reddere, reddidi, redditum	to give back, return
*redeo, redire, redii	to return, come back again
redigo, redigere, redegi, redactum	to reduce down
refert, referre, retulit (impersonal)	it matters (+ dative)
*relinquo, relinquere, reliqui, relictum	to allow (I.1.52)
*res, rei, f	thing, matter, foodstuff (II.2.71), property (II.2.106)
reticulum -i, n	bag
*retineo, retinere, retinui, retentum	to keep
*rex, regis, m	king
rhombus -i, m	turbot
rideo, ridere, risi, risum	to laugh

*ripa -ae, f	riverbank
risus -ūs, m	laughing-stock
*rogo, rogare, rogavi, rogatum	to summon, fetch
Romanus -a -um	Roman
ruo, ruere, rui, rutum	to fall down, collapse
*rursus (adverb)	back again
*rus, ruris, n	countryside
rusticus -a -um	rustic
saccus -i, m	bag
sacer, sacra, sacrum	sacred
*saepe	often
sal, salis, m	salt
salvus -a -um	healthy
sancio, sancire, sanxi, sanctum	to enact
sanus -a -um	sound, sensible
*sapiens, sapientis	wise
*satis	enough
scarus -i, m	parrot-wrasse fish
scaurus -a -um	having swollen ankles
*se	himself, herself, itself, themselves
sector, sectari, sectatus sum	to chase after
*secum	along with itself
securis -is, f	axe
*sed	but
sedeo, sedere, sedi, sessum	to sit well, stay in place
*semper	always
senectus, senectutis, f	old age
*senex, senis, m	old man
sensu	see **communis sensus**
*sequor, sequi, secutus sum	to pursue
sermo, sermonis, m	conversation, chattering
serpens, serpentis, m	snake

*servo, servare, servavi, servatum	to preserve
*servus -i, m	slave
*sese	= se
*seu ... seu ...	whether ... or ...
*seu	or else
sextarius -i, m	half a litre
*si	if
si modo	if only, provided that
si quis	if somebody
sibilo, sibilare, sibilavi, sibilatum	to hiss at
*sic	thus, in this way
siccus -a -um	dry (i.e. thirsty)
*sicut	just like
simplex	frank, outspoken (I.3.52), unsophisticated (II.2.73)
simplicior (comparative of simplex)	unembarrassed
*simul (ac)	as soon as (I.1.36, II.2.73–4), at the same time (I.1.58)
sincerus -a -um	clean
*sine (+ ablative)	without
Sisyphus -i, m	Sisyphus (I.3.47)
sitiens, sitientis	thirsty
*sive ... seu ...	whether ... or ...
*soleo, solere, solitus sum (+ infinitive)	to be in the habit of
*solus -a -um	alone
sopor, soporis, m	sleep
sordidus -a -um	dirty, squalid
sors, sortis, f	lot, destiny
spectaculum -i, n	display, show
*sperno, spernere, sprevi, spretum	to reject
stomachus -i, m	stomach

strabo, strabonis, m	a person who squints
struo, struere, struxi, structum	to build, construct
***studium** -i, n	enthusiasm
stupeo, stupere, stupui	to be dazed, astonished
suavis -e	pleasant
***sub** (+ ablative)	just before (I.1.10), under (I.3.34)
sudo, sudare, sudavi, sudatum	to sweat
***summus -a-um**	highest, utmost
***sumo, sumere, sumpsi, sumptum**	to take
superbus -a -um	scornful
***supero, superare, superavi, superatum**	to be left over, to remain
supremus -a -um	last, final
***surgo, surgere, surrexi, surrectum**	to get up
suscito, suscitare, suscitavi, suscitatum	to restore to health
tabella -ae, f	picture
***tacitus -a -um**	silent
talus -i, m	ankle
***tam … quam**	as … as (I.3.26–7)
***tamen**	yet, on the other hand (II.2.82)
tamquam	just as if
Tantalus -i, m	Tantalus (I.1.68)
tantulus -a -um	only so much, such a little amount
tantundem, tantidem, n	just as much
***tantus -a -um**	so much, so great
tardius (comparative adverb from **tardus**)	rather late
tardus -a -um	slow (I.3.58), sluggish (II.2.88)
tellus, telluris, f	earth
temere (adverb)	rashly

*templum -i, n	temple
tempto, temptare, temptavi, temptatum	to afflict
*tempus, temporis, n	time
tenuis -e	simple, modest
tenuo, tenuare, tenuavi, tenuatum	to make thin
tergeo, tergere, tersi, tersum	to rub (II.2.24)
tero, terere, trivi, tritum	to thresh (I.1.45)
*terra -ae, f	earth, land
timidus -a -um	scared, frightened
toga -ae, f	toga
*tollo, tollere, sustuli, sublatum	to remove
tondeo, tondere, totondi, tonsum	to cut one's hair
tracto, tractare, tractavi, tractatum	to treat, handle
*traho, trahere, traxi, tractum	to drag, pull
transcurro, transcurrere, transcurri, transcursum	to move quickly from one thing to another
Trausius -i, m	Trausius (II.2.99)
*tres, tria (dative: tribus)	three
truculentus -a -um	aggressive
trutina -ae, f	balance, scales
*tu, tui	you (*singular*)
tuber, tuberis, n	tumour
*tulisset	see **fero**
*tumultus -i, m	commotion
turbo, turbare, turbavi, turbatum	to churn up, make muddy
turdus -i, m	thrush
turpis -e	ugly, repellent
*tutus -a -um	safe, secure
*tuus -a -um	your (*singular*)

Tyndarides -ae, f	a descendant of Tyndareus (I.1.100)
***ubi**	where, when
umerus, umeri, m	shoulder
Ummidius -i, m	Ummidius (I.1.95)
***umquam**	ever
***unā**	together with, along with
***unda -ae**, f	wave
***unde**	from where?
***undique**	from everywhere
***unus, una, unum**	sole, alone
***urbs, urbis**, f	city
urgeo, urgere, ursi	to beset
urna -ae, f	urn, vessel
uro, urere, ussi, ustum	to burn
usquam	anywhere
usus -ūs, m	usefulness
***ut**	that (I.1.1), just as (I.1.46), so that, as (I.1.64)
ut ... si	as if
***uter**	which of the two?
utinam	if only, would that!
***utor, uti, usus sum** (+ ablative)	I use up
***uxor, uxoris**, f	wife
vades dare	to provide bail (I.1.11)
***valeo, valere, valui, valitum**	to be good for something (I.1.73), to be healthy (II.2.71)
valetudo, valetudinis, f	health
***validus -a -um**	strong, healthy
vanus -a -um	vain, hollow, illusory
varius -a -um	varied, different
varus -a -um	knock-kneed

vas, vasis, n	wine-jar
vectigal, vectigalis, n	revenues
vegetus -a -um	vigorous
*****veho, vehere, vexi, vectum**	to carry
*****vel**	or
velox, velocis	swift
*****veluti**	just like, for example
venalis -e	available for sale, slave (I.1.47)
veneo, venire, venii, venitum	to be sold
venia -ae, f	pardon, indulgence
*****venio, venire, veni, ventum**	to come
venter, ventris, m	belly
*****verbum -i**, n	word
verruca -ae, f	wart
versor, versari, versatus sum	to be engaged in
*****verto, vertere, verti, versum**	to turn
verum (conjunction)	but
*****verus -a -um**	true
vescor, vesci (+ ablative)	to feed on
vestio, vestire, vesti(v)i, vestitum	to clothe
vicinus -a -um	neighbour
*****victoria -ae**, f	victory
victus -ūs, m	livelihood, means of sustenance
*****video, videre, vidi, visum**	to see
*****videor, videri, visus sum**	to seem
vigeo, vigere, vigui	to thrive
vigilo, vigilare, vigilavi, vigilatum	to stay awake
vilis -is	cheap, of low value
vinum -i, n	wine
*****vir -i**, m	man

*virtus, virtutis, f	virtue, good quality
*vita -ae, f	life
vitio, vitiare, vitiavi, vitiatum	to spoil, to cause (food) to go bad
vitium -i, n	fault, defect, vice (II.2.21, II.2.78)
*vivo, vivere, vixi, victum	to live
*vix	not easily, with difficulty
*voco, vocare, vocavi, vocatum	to call
*volo, velle, volui	to wish, want
voluptas, voluptatis, f	pleasure
*vox, vocis, f	voice